The Urban
Labor Market

David Lewin
Raymond Horton
Robert Shick
Charles Brecher

foreword by
Eli Ginzberg

Conservation of Human Resources Studies—
Columbia University

The Praeger Special Studies program—utilizing the most modern and efficient book production techniques and a selective worldwide distribution network—makes available to the academic, government, and business communities significant, timely research in U.S. and international economic, social, and political development.

The Urban Labor Market

Institutions, Information, Linkages

PRAEGER SPECIAL STUDIES IN U.S. ECONOMIC, SOCIAL, AND POLITICAL ISSUES

Praeger Publishers   New York   Washington   London

Library of Congress Cataloging in Publication Data

Main entry under title:

The Urban labor market.

  (Praeger special studies in U.S. economic, social, and political issues)
  Includes bibliographical references.
  1. Labor supply—New York (City) 2. Manpower policy—New York (City) I. Lewin, David, 1943-
II. Title.
HD5726.N5U73   331.1'2'097471   74-14045
ISBN 0-275-09680-7

PRAEGER PUBLISHERS
111 Fourth Avenue, New York, N.Y. 10003, U.S.A.
5, Cromwell Place, London SW7 2JL, England

Published in the United States of America in 1974
by Praeger Publishers, Inc.

Printed in the United States of America

This report was prepared for the Manpower Administration, U.S. Department of Labor, under research number 70-34-70-04 authorized by Title I of the Manpower Development and Training Act. Since contractors performing research under government sponsorship are encouraged to express their own judgment freely, the report does not necessarily represent the department's official opinion or policy. Moreover, the contractor is solely responsible for the factual accuracy of all material developed in the report.

Reproduction in whole or in part permitted for any purpose of the United States government.

The Conservation of Human Resources Project, Columbia University, is an interdisciplinary research group now in its fourth decade of working in the field of human resources and manpower. Its investigations cover a broad spectrum with primary emphasis on the role of human resources in the economic development of the United States but including also other advanced economies and the developing world. In recent years the Conservation Project has increasingly focused on metropolitan labor markets. The Project also engages in research in health policy issues. Professor Eli Ginzberg, 525 Uris, Columbia University, New York, New York 10027, is director of the Project.

FOREWORD
by Eli Ginzberg

This collaborative study by four members of the Conservation of Human Resources Project, Columbia University, grows out of earlier work of the Project in urban economics and labor market information systems. In particular it extends the effort at conceptualization outlined by Boris Yavitz and Dean W. Morse in *The Labor Market: An Information System* (New York: Praeger, 1973), in which attention was focused on the importance of "intermediaries" in the preparation, processing, distribution, and use of manpower information by agents other than the employer who needs workers and the applicant in search of a job.

The present study appraises three types of intermediaries at different levels of the labor market—correctional institutions, vocational schools, and macroinstitutions, such as municipal government and trade unions. The authors address the critical question of the potential role of improved labor market information in facilitating the development and utilization of the skills and competences of the individuals and groups on which these intermediaries impinge. Throughout their analysis the authors seek to place the input of more and improved labor market information into a broader decision-making matrix in which a great many other variables operate to affect outcomes—variables such as the characteristics of job applicants, employer policies and practices, power relations among labor market participants, and the availability of jobs.

The production and use of labor market information involves the expenditure of resources. Therefore, the bromide that the functioning of complex urban labor markets can be improved by more and better information is not necessarily a useful guide for public or private action; it simplistically overlooks such critical questions as, What additional information should be collected? By whom should it be collected? Who is to cover the costs? And what real individual or social gains can be anticipated if more information is fed into the decision-making process?

It is one thing merely to take note of the need to develop "a comprehensive system of labor market information on a national, state, local, or other appropriate basis which shall be made publicly available in a timely fashion," as the Congress did in both its 1968 amendments to the Manpower Development and Training Act and in its recently enacted Comprehensive Employment and Training Act of 1973 (sec. 312 [a]). It is something else again to spell out the implications of such a comprehensive system. Yavitz and Morse were the first to address that question in a general way; Lewin and his associates talk specifically to this issue.

The principal aim of this foreword is to sketch for the reader the manner in which the authors explore the role of improved labor market information in discrete urban settings and to precipitate a few generalizations that flow from their analysis.

David Lewin, in his account of the flow of persons through correctional institutions, a prototypical analysis of institutionalized populations, calls attention to the modest contribution that improved information can make to manpower development and utilization among this group in the face of the constraints operating to keep most released prisoners in, at best, peripheral jobs. Among the constraints to which Lewin directs the reader's attention are the inadequacies in the preparation for and experience in the world of work characteristic of most persons when they enter prison. The vast majority are undereducated, have acquired few skills, have held only marginal jobs; in short, when they enter prison they are ill-prepared for employment and income-earning activities.

Since few prisons have been able to structure effective educational and occupational training programs, and since most work opportunities for prisoners are limited to relatively simple housekeeping chores and include only a small number of white-collar positions in the office, the library, and the laboratory, most prisoners at the time of their release are ill-equipped to make their way in a competitive market, particularly because of the pervasive discrimination against them, but also because of the many ways that imprisonment itself promotes behaviors that are dysfunctional for coping with labor markets subsequent to release.

With little skill or work experience to offer a prospective employer, and carrying the stigmata of having been convicted and served time, most released prisoners need special assistance in locating a job with which they can cope and that promises to enable them to become self-supporting. Clearly, an up-to-date listing of employers who are willing to hire ex-convicts and a specification of available jobs, together with the wages and other conditions of employment, would be of real assistance to released prisoners. But such information is not currently being collected by any public or private agency, and it is questionable whether it could be collected. Even an employer who is willing occasionally to hire a former prisoner on the advice of a trusted individual or agency would think twice about agreeing to broadcast his willingness to employ ex-prisoners. As long as most preferred positions in the labor market are closed to ex-prisoners, it is difficult to see what improved labor market information, per se, can contribute to their employability. The critical lack is not information but jobs. To assume that the latter can be overcome by more of the former is to deny reality. This helps to explain why Lewin concludes that the critical need of ex-prisoners in reentering the labor market is job placement and support. Improved labor market information can make at best a minimal contribution. The real need for parolees is expanded employment services linked to suitable jobs in the private and public sectors.

The second analysis, undertaken by Robert Shick and Charles Brecher, focuses on vocational schools in New York City and consequently involves a much broader consideration of the interfacing of information and the labor market. Although their primary focus is on the public vocational high school, the authors take cognizance of the wide variety of occupational training institutions in New York City that characterize vocational programs in academic high schools, community colleges, and private technical institutions. They estimate that about 850,000 individuals underwent one or another type of occupational training in New York City in 1970-71, a staggering figure even when juxtaposed against a total labor force of about 4 million. They explore the extent to which the wide range of training institutions have access to and make use of labor market information to shape their curricula and guide their students, and they conclude that on balance the flow of information about changing trends in the world of work has had at most a minor impact.

They found, for instance, that throughout the 1960s only two new curricula had been introduced into the city's vocational high schools, primarily reflecting the bureaucratic difficulties of bringing about changes in an arena characterized by a teaching staff with tenure and space and equipment that could not readily be altered. Further, they found that the two principal agencies involved in the preparation of labor market information, the Regional Office of the U.S. Department of Labor and the New York State Employment Service, are in no position to provide reliable guidance about the number of job openings that develop in different occupational fields as young people complete their studies and become available for work. While their gross projections about the total level of employment and the number of job openings proved reliable, the more specific estimates of these agencies, occupation by occupation, industry by industry, were often unreliable. The responsible school officials, therefore, relied heavily on their own sources for clues about the likelihood of job-availability in various fields. Moreover, the authors note that the individual student seeks guidance for shaping his educational and career plans largely from his family, friends, and peers.

Shick and Brecher also found that the introduction of "open enrollment" into the CUNY system at the beginning of the 1970s, which guarantees admission for every high school graduate to either a public senior or community college, reduced, if it did not eliminate, considerations of employability for different vocational curricula. Since the majority of those who completed their courses of study did not enter the labor market directly but sought and gained admission to college, the criterion of how well their high school education prepared them for the world of work was largely irrelevant; the critical question was how well they were prepared for college.

The authors are careful not to downgrade the contribution that better information can make to improving the education and career choices not only of high school graduates who go on to college but also of those who terminate their education after receiving their diplomas, others who drop out without obtaining their diplomas, and those who begin to continue their studies after a period of time during which they have worked, served in the military, or merely passed time. The authors state that the information that would be most helpful to these groups would help them keep their options open and would facilitate their moving among school, work, military service, marriage, homemaking, and nonwork activities—a pattern characteristic of increasing numbers of young people. But they also note that better information will not suffice. Young people need access to guidance, counseling, and placement services to help them find their way through the maze of loosely articulated schools and the even greater maze of job opportunities in New York City. Consequently, as does Lewin in his study, Shick and Brecher recommend strengthening supportive institutions.

The third study, set out in Chapters 6 and 7 by Raymond Horton, focuses on the extent to which improved labor market information is likely to aid the decision-making processes of the principal actors—employers, trade unions, and municipal government. Particular attention is paid to the ways in which local government relates to the local economy via employment, education, manpower training, economic development, and the provision of services.

Horton makes a series of critical observations about the nature of the informational process before exploring the advantages of strengthening it. He notes basic considerations: for example, since information is power, in any conflict situation (for example, collective bargaining), each side devotes much of its effort to collecting and analyzing information not readily available to the other. He also reminds the reader though that since many decisions lie within the political arena (for example, whether to build a new convention center or to construct an expressway), the role of information is marginal because the important factors are the interests and goals of the groups that can be combined into a winning political coalition. Horton also reminds the reader that when and where particular interest groups need critical information (for example, department stores that require wage and fringe benefit data, or the construction unions' monitoring of the changing demands for and supplies of skilled workers) these large intermediaries have specialized ways of obtaining the information they desire.

Horton also analyzes in some detail the extent to which the fractionalization of city government interferes with the effective collection and evaluation of labor market information by the several quasi-independent municipal agencies and particularly the unwillingness of these agencies to share the information they have garnered with other departments of the city government, believing that they derive some special advantages, if only of a putative nature, by holding unto themselves data that others do not have.

Despite these and other caveats about slippage between improved information and improved decision making by the principal intermediaries, Horton does not draw a negative conclusion about the potential contribution that improved labor market information can make to a complex economy like New York's. He stresses the dynamic nature of the New York labor market and the desirability of the principals' staying abreast of the important changes under way. But, like his co-authors, he is aware of the reality that, the acquiring of improved information being costly, the effort's worth depends on how it will be put to use. Once again it is concluded that information by itself is not the answer, but more and better information fed into and used by major institutions to improve their manpower dimensions can represent an important advance.

The foregoing pages have merely suggested the rich coverage and analysis that characterize the three levels at which the cooperating authors have explored the potentiality of improved information to strengthen the urban labor market. To frame the total effort, Lewin has written a long introduction that sets forth the present state of labor market information and also provides a succinct summary of the basic characteristics of the New York labor market, the laboratory for the present investigation. The work is further enriched by the concluding chapter, also drafted by Lewin, in which the reader is provided with a summary of findings and particularly of the critical issues that should be further explored so that the role of information in the urban labor market can be optimized.

One conclusion emerges with clarity. The strengthening of the informational base must go hand in hand with the strengthening of the decision making of key labor market principals. When progress occurs on both fronts, we can look forward to significant improvements in the development and utilization of the nation's human resources. Better information alone cannot result in significant progress, but better information linked to a stronger network of labor market institutions that use the improved information for improving their decision making will result in gains to the individual, the intermediaries, and the urban economy.

CONTENTS

Page

FOREWORD by Eli Ginzberg   vi

LISTS OF TABLES AND FIGURES   xiv

Chapter

1   INTRODUCTION   1

    Conceptual Foundations of Labor Market Information   1
    Government and Labor Market Information   5
    The New York City Labor Market   8
       Employment Trends   10
       Population and Labor Force Characteristics   14
       Pay and Price Trends   15
    Microstudies of Labor Market Information   19
    Notes   23

2   MANPOWER SERVICES FOR OFFENDERS:
    THE INSTITUTIONAL DYNAMIC   28

    Manpower Services for the Institutionalized   29
    Modeling the Institutionalization Process   37
       Characteristics of the Institutionalized   37
       Institutionalization and Its Impact   38
       Post-release Experiences   39
       Labor Market Functioning   40
       Hiring and Selection Practices   40
    Summary   41
    Notes   45

3   INFORMATIONAL FLOWS AND LABOR MARKET
    INTERMEDIARIES FOR THE INSTITUTIONALIZED   49

    Correctional Institutions and the Institutionalized in
      New York City   50
    Labor Market Imperatives and the Formerly
      Institutionalized   54
    Margins of Search and Labor Market Surrogates   58
    The Intermediaries   59
       Family and Friends   59

        Probation and Parole Officers   60
        Community Institutions   62
    Inmate Manpower Utilization in Correctional Institutions   64
        Compensation   65
        Work Scheduling   66
        Mobility   67
        Due Process   68
    Summary   71
    Notes   71

4   PUBLIC OCCUPATIONAL TRAINING AND LABOR
    MARKET INFORMATION   76

    Occupational Training Agencies   76
    Labor Market Information: Desirable and Available   86
    The Uses of Available Labor Market Information   95
    Conclusions   97
    Notes   97

5   IMPROVED INFORMATION FOR STUDENT DECISIONS   100

    Educational Decisions   100
    Information for Student Decisions   102
    Decision Patterns in New York City   104
    Implications for Information Services   108
    Notes   111

6   THE MAJOR LABOR MARKET INSTITUTIONS IN
    NEW YORK CITY   112

    The Principal Nongovernmental Actors   113
        Employing Institutions   114
        Unions   116
    The City Government   118
    Linkages between the City Government and the Economy   120
    Notes   127

7   LABOR MARKET INFORMATION IN NEW YORK   129

    The Existing Stock of Labor Market Information   130
        Information Gaps   131
        Dated Information   132
        Poor Quality   132
        Contradictory Data   133
        Dissemination of Data   133
    Toward an Improved Labor Market Information System   136
    The Potential of Improved Labor Market Information   137

Chapter   Page

        Continuing Research in Urban Labor Market Information   141
        Notes   144

8   CONCLUSIONS AND POLICY RECOMMENDATIONS   145

        Notes   154

ABOUT THE AUTHORS   156

LIST OF TABLES AND FIGURES

Table   Page

1.1   Percent Change in Wage and Salary Employment, United States
       and New York City, 1969-72   9

1.2   Industrial Distribution of Wage and Salary Employment, New
       York City, 1972   10

1.3   Changes in Industrial Composition of Employment, New York
       City, 1950-72   11

1.4   Leading Industries of Job Change, New York City, 1959-72   13

1.5   Occupational Distribution of Employed, New York City, 1970   14

1.6   Occupational Distribution of Employed, by Ethnic Group,
       New York City, 1960 and 1970   16

1.7   Percent Increases in Earnings and Consumer Prices, United
       States and New York City, 1969-72   18

2.1   Inmates of Correctional and Delinquency Institutions, United
       States and New York State, 1970   29

3.1   Inmates in N.Y.C. Department of Correction Institutions and
       County Jails Located in New York City, by Status and
       Institution, December 31, 1970   51

3.2   Inmates under Custody in N.Y.S. Correctional Institutions, by
       Reason for Commitment and Sex, December 31, 1970   52

3.3   Number of Inmates under Custody in Correctional Institutions,
       by Institution and Sex, December 31, 1964-71   56

4.1   Graduates of New York City High Schools, June 1971   78

4.2   Enrollment by Trade Area of Tenth- through Twelfth-Grade
       Students at Vocational High Schools, 1960 and 1970   79

4.3   Matriculated Students at CUNY Community Colleges, by
       Field, Fall 1970   81

4.4   Bachelor's and First Professional Degrees Granted by Colleges
       and Universities in New York City, 1960-61 and 1970-71   82

4.5   Enrollment for Advanced Degrees (Excluding First Professional
       Degrees) at Universities, 1960-61 and 1970-71   84

xiv

Table		Page
4.6	Training Opportunities in Public Manpower Programs in New York City, FY 1970/71	85
4.7	Actual and Projected Employment in New York City, by Industry, 1970	90
5.1	Enrollment and Diplomas for a Cohort of Tenth Graders in New York City Public Schools, 1967-70	104
5.2	Percent of High School Graduates Continuing Education Full Time, New York City, 1970 and 1971	106
5.3	Choice of College among New York City Graduates Attending College, 1970 and 1971	107

Figures

2.1	Flow Model of the Institutionalization Process	42
5.1	Decision Outcomes for a Cohort of New York City Tenth Graders	105

The Urban
Labor Market

1

INTRODUCTION

This book examines the role, uses, and function of labor market information in the urban environment. Our effort, a study focusing on New York City, explores the ways in which labor market information enters into the decision-making processes of governments, educational institutions, and former occupants of incarcerative institutions. The inquiry was sparked (a) by the considerable attention recently paid to labor market operations and the role of information in facilitating smoothly functioning labor markets and (b) by the relative paucity of knowledge about the utilization of labor market information in the real world, especially the large urban areas in which so much of the United States' economic activity is concentrated. Informed judgments about labor market information require additional knowledge of the ways in which such information is actually used in contemporary urban society.

CONCEPTUAL FOUNDATIONS OF LABOR MARKET INFORMATION

As Cartter and Marshall have noted, the concept of a labor market is an abstraction referring "merely to the area within which exchanges frequently take place."[1] Exchanges occur between those who demand and those who supply labor in markets that are local, regional, national, or even international in scope. As Reynolds notes, the boundaries of a particular labor market are established by buyers and sellers whose communication is sufficiently close to cause the price of labor "to be the same throughout the area."[2]

This conceptualization of a labor market flows from the competitive model grounded in classical price theory. In a purely competitive labor market, wages allocate labor (employment) in such a way that the market tends toward

1

equilibrium. Employers hiring the same type of labor in this market offer the same wage rates, having neither the need to offer more nor the possibility of paying less. Wage differences between occupations in the purely competitive market will reflect only the net of advantages or disadvantages accruing to the occupations.[3] Following Smith, wages will vary with (a) the agreeableness of employment, (b) the cost of learning the business, (c) the constancy of employment, (d) the trust to be reposed in the worker, and (e) the probability of success in the occupation.[4] Interoccupational wage differentials based on factors other than those enumerated above will be eliminated as workers seeking to maximize comparative net advantage move away from low-paying to higher-paying occupations. Similarly, geographic wage differentials (except for equalizing differentials) will also tend to be eliminated.

A view of labor markets based upon the competitive model requires fundamental assumptions about the number of buyers and sellers, freedom of exchange, the level of employment (or unemployment), and utility maximization. These assumptions, known well by those familiar with neoclassical price theory, need not be adumbrated here. Perhaps the most crucial of these assumptions, however, certainly the one most relevant for purposes of this study, concerns knowledge of market conditions:

> Workers have full information about job vacancies, wages, and other terms of employment in each occupation and employing unit. They also have full freedom of choice.
> Employers have full and accurate information on the cost of hiring additional labor, and on how much this labor will add to their output.[5]

In the conventional price theoretic model, then, labor market information is not only assumed to be abundantly available and widely dispersed, but required for the efficient functioning of (competitive) labor markets.

That the conditions requisite to purely competitive labor (or product) markets are not necessarily or even generally present in the real world is by now well established. For example, Stigler found substantial wage dispersion—that is variation in employer wage offers—for virtually homogeneous labor in a local labor market and suggested that wage dispersion is even larger in more heterogeneous labor markets.[6] Such dispersion occurs because the complete knowledge required to effectuate a single price (wage) is seldom possessed as "it costs more to learn of alternative prices (wages) than (at the margin) this information yields."[7] The individual worker will search for higher wages, a critical facet of labor market information, until the marginal costs of search equal the marginal gain in wages. For the employer, wages and search costs are substitutes; the more efficient the employer is in finding high-quality workers, the less he need pay (in search costs) for them.[8]

More recently, Alchian has noted that economic theory can be formulated so that shortages, surpluses, unemployment, queues, idle resources, and non-price rationing are consistent with price stability.[9] The key analytical point is that "collating information about potential exchange opportunities is costly and can be performed in various ways."[10] The notion of costless information, an apparent postulate of formalized price theory, is thus analytically vacuous. Labor market information can be acquired only at a cost, though institutions such as state employment services or private employment agencies presumably facilitate and economize on the search process.[11]

Concepts of information and search provide the underpinnings for contemporary macro- and microeconomic analyses of labor market behavior. For example, Holt's conceptualization of the labor market emphasizes the stocks and flows of both jobs and workers.[12] The unemployed and some who are employed search the labor market for job opportunities, or more precisely, information about job vacancies, adjusting their wage aspirations as further information is gained. Similarly, employers search the market for workers, adjusting their wage offers in response to additional information about the labor supply. In this dynamic model, there is considerable flow through or turnover among the stock of job vacancies and unemployed workers. The magnitude of these stocks and flows and the volume of search activity engaged in by demanders and suppliers of labor depends upon the level of aggregate economic activity.

Following the general outlines of this model, Holt proposes that public policy be directed towards facilitating search and information-seeking processes.[13] While there are a variety of ways in which this directive might be carried out, the provision of more and higher-quality information would presumably not only facilitate the efficient functioning of labor markets through the removal of structural impediments but would also have a salutory effect on the rate of price change. Thus manpower policies directed at job search and information presumably can be used to deal with problems of both unemployment and inflation.

In the construction of this model and in their policy prescriptions, Holt and his colleagues apparently accept the existence of the so-called Phillips' relation, specifying a tradeoff between the economywide rate of inflation and the level of unemployment.[14] Obviously, such a tradeoff presents the policy maker with a dilemma, since the best of both worlds—that is, stable prices and only frictional unemployment—is operationally unattainable.

While we do not attempt to resolve the issue of the Phillips' relation in this study, we may note that the policy prescriptions of those who adhere to the notion of a natural rate of unemployment[15] are similar to those forwarded by advocates of the inflation-unemployment tradeoff.[16] Both groups call for a greater flow of information (for example, about job vacancies or going wage rates) as an integral part of manpower policies designed to reduce unemployment and improve the functioning of labor markets. This would cause a shift to the left (in a graphical portrayal) of either the Phillips relation or the long-run vertical supply curve of labor representing the natural rate of unemployment. Following Killingsworth, these measures are designed to deal primarily with structural inefficiencies in labor markets.[17]

In a recent work, Yavitz and Morse offer a systemic view of labor market information in preference to "the conventional economic model of an employer/employee exchange which appears far too narrow, static and oversimplified."[18] Underlying this analysis is the notion of a transaction in the job market resulting from a complex series of processes and flows. The systems

3

approach not only facilitates identification of the various elements in the labor market dynamic, but also provides for clarification of their functions and the tracing of their interrelationships.

Like Holt, these authors identify prospective employees and job vacancies as the major components of the job market.[19] Going further, however, Yavitz and Morse delineate the critical intermediaries in the informational system whose actions "significantly modify the flows and arrivals of the two main inputs into the job market."[20] Major intermediaries include (a) those impacting directly on the market—friends and relations, employment agencies, and data banks; (b) those principally influencing the manpower side of the system—guidance and curriculum planning; (c) those influencing the employment side—employer's planning; and (d) those affecting the entire range of the system—unions and government policy.[21] Thus, increases in the efficiency of labor markets may result not only from enlarging the amount of information made directly available to employers and job seekers but also from improving the performance of labor market intermediaries.

These labor market models are general in nature, of course, and for this reason, perhaps, tend to imply a certain homogeneity of behavior on the part of labor market participants. Yet it would seem that urban labor markets are increasingly heterogeneous. This heterogeneity is particularly true of New York City, where differences in education, skill, and income levels between racial and ethnic groups, and the changing composition of the city's population, labor force, and occupational structure pose challenges to the urban (and metro-politan) economy. To what extent do the city's employers draw upon a labor supply from the larger metropolitan area? Is the urban transportation system able to facilitate the employment of large numbers of suburbanites in the central city? Alternatively, will employers move away from the central city in response to changes in the distribution and composition of the labor supply? If city residents are not prepared for the expanding employment sectors, how and where will they be employed? Will they in fact be active labor force partici-pants or, instead, pursue nonmarket alternatives?[22] If the less-skilled, less-educated, and low-income persons remain in the labor force, what are the implications for the functioning of labor markets and, relatedly, the utilization of labor market information? All of these questions indicate that information costs may be relatively high and the search process relatively complex in the urban economy.

To summarize, contemporary models of labor market operations empha-size concepts of job search and information, and their attendant behavioral implications. These models differ from, though are not necessarily inconsistent with, the concept of a purely competitive labor market derived from neo-classical price theory. Further, though these models specify general patterns of labor market behavior, the complexities of urban economies may cause pecu-liarities in the functioning of urban labor markets and, relatedly, utilization of labor market information. Finally, because of their emphasis on the process of exchange, current labor market models have implications for the role of government in the provision of labor market information and in facilitating search activity. We now consider some of these implications.

4

Probably the main thrust of current thinking about labor markets and the role of government is toward improving the matching of demands for and supplies of labor. Government is assigned a large role in achieving this goal because it is able to serve as a repository of knowledge about job opportunities and prospective employees. By actively disseminating such information, government presumably would enable employers to fill their vacancies and workers to secure jobs. Labor Markets would thus function more efficiently, contributing to the economic and social (to say nothing of the political) welfare of the country.[23]

The notion of governmentally-assisted job matching does not, of course, represent entirely "new thought" in the area of labor markets; instead, this objective may be more readily attainable now than previously, given the pattern of recent technological developments. In particular, the evolution of computer technology has greatly accentuated the emphasis on matching processes in labor markets.[24] Terms, such as "computer-assisted placement," "job inventories," "data banks," and so on, are now part of the language of this subject, with the federal government being among the strongest supporters of computer-based data banks.[25] Yet the emergence of an analytical tool, even one with the widespread appeal of electronic data processing, neither obviates the conceptual underpinnings of labor market behavior nor solves the operational problems attendant upon attempts to improve the efficiency of labor markets.

Since the Wagner-Peyser Act of 1933 the United States has operated the Federal-State Employment Service (ES), which, as its title suggests, is supposed to provide job-seekers with knowledge of job opportunities and employers with prospective candidates for employment. The labor market matching concept was thus given explicit support in public policy well before the advent of more specific governmental manpower programs or of computer technology. Yet virtually all observers have remarked on the inability of the ES to aid the operation of labor markets in a truly meaningful way.[26] While analysts differ about the relative importance of factors accounting for the limited effectiveness of the ES, they commonly note the difficulties of trying to operate an employment matching system when no mechanism exists for systematically obtaining job vacancy data. For example, the federal government has never required that private employers list their job openings with the ES, though a recent executive order providing for mandatory vacancy reporting by government contractors may considerably increase "the number of highly skilled and better paying job openings to which the ES could thereafter refer clients."[27] Whether the values and sentiments now dominant in the United States support a general policy of compulsory job vacancy listing (or more active labor market policies) is problematic, and, lacking such data, whatever the advances in models of labor market behavior or computer technology, the problems of effectuating more efficiently functioning labor markets will remain.[28]

5

As another example, we might consider the issue of formal versus informal channels of labor market information. Those who criticize labor markets for being inefficient, irrational, and disorderly invariably propose creation of a formal labor exchange to improve their operation. Presumably, participants in the labor market will avail themselves of formal sources of information in preference to any other type. Yet this assumption is challenged by microstudies of labor market behavior showing how buyers and sellers of labor actually carry on search activity.[29] These studies indicate that the operation of local labor markets cannot be considered analogous to that of commodity exchanges.[30] In the latter, the kind of information required is extensive rather than intensive. In contrast, "the problem facing the employer and job seeker is not to get in touch with the largest number of potential applicants (employers); rather, it is to find a few applicants (employers) promising enough to be worth the investment of thorough investigation."[31] The operational and informational characteristics of job markets thus more closely resemble used car markets than they do commodity markets. Since it "seems to be inherently easier for governmental agencies to provide information in the extensive rather than intensive dimension,"[32] governmental informational programs may exacerbate rather than alleviate inefficiencies in labor market search processes.

Still another issue that emerges in connection with labor market information is the timing of government information efforts and, more generally, manpower programs. A review of American manpower legislation reveals that some important governmental efforts in this area occurred during and in response to periods of economic stagnation. This applies to Wagner-Peyser, but more particularly to manpower programs legislated during the early 1960s—the Area Redevelopment Act (ARA), the Manpower Development and Training Act (MDTA), and the Economic Opportunity Act (EOA). Each of these acts, though most clearly MDTA, was intended to improve the quality of the labor supply by offering remedial, basic, vocational, and skill training and, to a considerably lesser degree, moving allowances and labor market information. Unfavorable economic conditions, then, triggered programs aimed at the labor supply. Indeed, this stimulus-response pattern underlies the Emergency Employment Act of 1971, in which the level of funds provided to state and local governments under the act's Public Employment Program is dependent upon national and regional unemployment rates.[33]

Some question the timing (if not the wisdom) of these policies. For example, Hammermesh suggests that when the economy is sluggish or in recession and loose labor markets obtain, government manpower programs have a displacement effect.[34] This effect occurs because subsidized workers provide employers with a source of labor that is cheap in relation to nonsubsidized sources. Accordingly, Hammermesh suggests adoption of an "anti-trigger" approach to manpower programs.[35] Instead of increasing investments in training, information, and counseling when unemployment rates are relatively high, as occurs under present programs, these labor market services should be provided—triggered—when unemployment is low. By alleviating true labor shortages and bottlenecks, manpower programs would serve to reduce inflationary pressures and thereby improve the operation of labor markets and provide real opportunities for those in the labor force. Thus, manpower

6

programs, including those concerned with the provision of labor market information, would be demand-oriented (or demand-and-supply-oriented) rather than strictly supply-oriented.[3][6]

Finally, another potentially important issue regarding labor market information concerns the use of that information by government, business, and labor for purposes of long-range economic planning. For example, city governments have been slow to acquire labor market information for use in the planning function, preferring instead to rely on information gathered by others. Caught as they are in midst of diverging local interests regarding developmental and manpower policies, city governments have often lacked the capacity and power to use what limited labor market information exists. Public education, the principal manpower program in any city, is characteristically conducted without close reference to local labor market conditions. This principle, if carried to the extreme, can negate the usefulness of certain important educational programs, particularly vocational education. Similarly, efforts by government to develop certain industrial or service sectors without proper reference to the quality or availability of a labor force make little sense. Labor market information and its utilization seem intertwined with the planning and development of an urban economy.

This discussion indicates that questions concerning the provision of labor market information and the role of government in the operation of a labor market information system are not settled. As noted above, there are important policy issues to be considered: Should employers be required to report job vacancies to government? Should manpower programs, including those pertaining specifically to information, be triggered by tight rather than loose labor markets, thereby operating as part of a comprehensive anti-inflation policy? Can labor market information play a useful role in helping government, business, and unions, to plan long-range development policies? Additionally, several operational questions need to be resolved: Should existing informational sources, particularly informal sources, be integrated within an overall labor market information system? Should information be targeted for direct participants in the labor market (that is, employers and job seekers) or, instead, aimed at labor market intermediaries? Should labor market information relevant to both long- and short-run conditions be provided, or should more emphasis be given to the latter? Finally, and perhaps most basically, does labor market information, particularly information that flows primarily from and deeply involves government, make a difference to participants in the labor market?

Responses to these questions, especially the last question, are not easily generated, notably because little knowledge exists concerning the relative value and use of labor market information. Lacking the appropriate empirical evidence, judgments about labor market information continue to rely on conviction, assumption, or assertion.

One way of dealing with this problem is to seek qualitative knowledge about the utilization of labor market information in selected labor markets. In concluding their conceptual work, Yavitz and Morse recommend the launching of one or more projects as part of the initial efforts of the Department of Labor in pursuing the development of a labor market information system. They note further that "the location of a pilot project deserves careful attention," and that they "believe that New York City should be included in any such project. . . ."[37]

Following this directive, we have undertaken an examination of the role, uses, and functioning of labor market information in the nation's most complex urban economy, New York City. The investigation consists of three distinct yet interrelated studies that focus on the utilization of labor market information by (a) correctional institutions—and their inmates—engaged in the dual processes of incarceration and rehabilitation; (b) educational and training institutions in the making of curricular and program decisions; (c) major actors in the city economy (that is, business, governments, and unions), but especially government manpower planners.

Each of these studies will be more fully described below. Initially, however, we present selected data about New York City that illustrate not only the complexity of its economy but also its attractiveness as a setting for investigating the uses and limits of labor market information.

THE NEW YORK CITY LABOR MARKET[38]

New York City is at once both typical and atypical of urban labor markets in the United States. Like other cities, it is affected by economic policies of the federal government and by cyclical changes in the national economy. It is distinguished from other cities, however, by (among other things) its size and by the severity of its reaction to aggregate economic trends.

For example, New York City's population is more than twice that of the nation's next largest city, Chicago, and, if taken separately, four of its five boroughs would rank third, fourth, sixth, and eighth, respectively, in size among all U.S. cities. Similarly, New York City's labor force exceeds Chicago's by well over 2 million persons, about the same magnitude by which it surpasses the entire Los Angeles-Long Beach Standard Metropolitan Statistical Area work force.[39]

In 1972 about 3.5 million wage and salary workers were employed in New York City; however, this employment level represents a decline of about 240,000 jobs since 1969. In merely this three-year span (1969-72), New York City lost approximately 85 percent of the jobs it had gained during the previous nine years (1960-69). Further, recent employment losses in the city were only slightly offset by job gains in the suburbs of New York. While employment in the United States, and in most metropolitan areas, was virtually stable during the economic recession of 1970-71, the city's employment declined by 3.5 percent (Table 1.1). In the generally expansionary 1971-72 period, when employment increased nationally by almost 3 percent, among the twenty largest metropolitan areas only New York and St. Louis experienced employment declines.[40]

The relative looseness of the New York City labor market in recent years is further illustrated by comparative unemployment data. Between 1968 and

8

TABLE 1.1

Percent Change in Wage and Salary
Employment, United States and New York City,
1969-72

Industry	Percent Change		
	1969-70	1970-71	1971-72
United States			
Total	0.4	0.1	2.8
Manufacturing	−4.1	−4.2	1.7
Private nonmanufacturing	2.1	1.4	3.2
Government	2.6	2.6	3.4
New York City			
Total	−1.4	−3.5	−2.0
Manufacturing	−7.2	−8.0	−3.2
Private nonmanufacturing	−0.4	−3.1	−1.9
Government	2.9	1.1	−1.0

Source: U.S. Department of Labor, Bureau of Labor Statistics, Middle Atlantic Regional Office, *1972 Year-End Report on Employment, Prices, and Earnings in New York City*, Regional Report No. 33 (Washington, D.C.: Government Printing Office, December 1972), p. 4.

1971, when unemployment increased nationally from 3.5 to 5.9 percent of the labor force, New York City's rate rose even more substantially, from 3.9 to 6.7 percent. In 1968 New York City had the second lowest unemployment rate among 14 of the nation's largest cities, but in 1971 seven of these cities had lower unemployment rates than New York's, even though they all experienced increased unemployment over the three-year period. The relative deterioration of New York's unemployment position was especially marked between 1970 and 1971, again indicating the strong impact of cyclical economic changes on the city's economy and labor market.

Recent employment declines in New York City should, of course, be viewed against the larger (and long-term) picture of the city as a complex, service-oriented urban economy of considerable, indeed surpassing, complexity. This perspective emerges more clearly in our discussion below. Suffice it to say that short-run changes in the city's economy, in this instance characterized by noticeable employment declines, should obfuscate neither the general richness and variety of economic activity and employment opportunity that it possesses nor the position of New York City as the most advanced, perhaps, of all service economies.[41]

9

Employment Trends

Perhaps the most outstanding characteristic of New York City's economy is its heavy service orientation. While two out of every three U.S. workers are employed in service-producing industries, in New York City the proportion is closer to four out of five (Table 1.2). Though New York City has traditionally had a more service-oriented economy than the rest of the nation, the difference has sharpened in recent years. Over the last two decades the proportion of New Yorkers employed in goods-producing industries declined even more rapidly than in the United States as a whole.

Since 1950 the major sectors of job expansion in New York City have been finance, insurance, and real estate (FIRE), services, and government (Table 1.3). Together, these industries added almost 550,000 jobs to the New York City economy between 1950 and 1972, about two thirds of this growth having occurred since 1960. Government employment, which accounted for

TABLE 1.2

Industrial Distribution of Wage and Salary
Employment, New York City, 1972

Industry	Number of Jobs	Percent
Total	3,542,900	100.0
Goods-producing	783,500	22.1
Manufacturing	683,800	19.3
Durables	211,300	6.0
Nondurables	472,500	13.3
Construction	99,000	2.8
Mining	900	.0*
Service-producing	2,759,200	77.9
Transportation and public utilities	297,100	8.4
Wholesale and retail trade	696,100	19.6
Finance, insurance, and real estate	449,000	12.7
Services	753,000	21.3
Government	564,000	15.9

*Less than .01 of one percent.

Source: U.S. Department of Labor, Bureau of Labor Statistics, Middle Atlantic Regional Office, *1972 Year-End Report on Employment, Prices, and Earnings in New York City*, Regional Report No. 33 (Washington, D.C.: Government Printing Office, December 1972), p. 6.

TABLE 1.3

Changes in Industrial Composition of Employment, New York City, 1950-72

Industry Division	Change in Number of Jobs			Percentage Change		
	1950-60	1960-72	1950-72	1950-60	1960-72	1950-72
Total	70,000	4,500	74,700	2.0	0.1	2.2
1. Manufacturing	- 92,100	-263,000	-355,100	- 8.9	-27.8	-34.2
Durables	- 7,400	- 92,300	- 99,700	- 2.4	-30.4	-32.1
Nondurables	- 84,700	-170,700	-255,400	-11.6	-26.5	-35.1
2. Contract construction	2,300	- 26,300	- 24,000	1.9	-21.0	-19.5
3. Mining	200	- 1,000	- 800	11.8	-47.4	-47.0
4. Transportation and public utilities	- 13,400	- 21,000	- 34,400	- 4.0	- 6.6	-10.4
5. Wholesale and retail trade	- 10,000	- 48,700	- 58,700	- 1.3	- 6.5	- 7.8
6. Finance, insurance and real estate	49,800	63,000	112,800	14.8	16.3	33.6
7. Services	99,600	145,700	245,300	19.6	24.0	48.3
8. Government	33,800	155,800	189,600	9.0	38.2	50.6
Industries 1-5	-113,000	-360,000	-473,000	- 5.0	-20.3	-21.0
Industries 6-8	183,200	364,500	547,700	15.0	26.0	45.0

Sources: Compiled from source cited for Table 1.1 and from U.S. Department of Labor, Bureau of Labor Statistics, Middle Atlantic Regional Office, *New York City in Transition: Population, Jobs, Prices and Pay in a Decade of Change,* Regional Report No. 34, (Washington, D.C.: Government Printing Office, July 1973), p. 23.

less than 11 percent of total employment in New York City in 1950 (and only 11.5 percent ten years later), grew more rapidly than any other industry over the next 22 years and now accounts for almost one of every six wage and salary positions in the city. Indeed, since 1959, local government has added more jobs than any other industry in New York City (Table 1.4).

In contrast to the pattern of employment growth in FIRE, services, and government between 1950 and 1972 stands the sharp reduction in jobs among all other major industry categories in New York City (Table 1.3). Employment in these industries declined by 473,000 (or 21 percent) over the 1950-72 period, with approximately three-fourths of the loss occurring since 1960. Manufacturing job losses were especially large, so that by 1972 little more than one in five of New York City's wage and salary workers was employed in manufacturing, compared with three of ten in 1950. As shown in Table 1.4, apparel manufacturing heads the list of declining industries in New York City. Interestingly, wholesale and retail trade, which remains the second largest employment sector in New York City, lost almost 8 percent of its jobs during the 1950-72 period. Again, most of this job-loss took place after 1960.

The pattern of employment changes in New York City may briefly be contrasted with that of the United States as a whole. Since 1950 the nation has experienced employment growth in every major industry category. In FIRE, services, and government—sectors in which New York City employment increased by 45 percent between 1950 and 1972—the rate of job increase nationally exceeded 100 percent. Moreover, while employment in all other major industries increased by 34 percent in the United States during this period, it declined by more than 20 percent in New York City. Consequently, the city's share of employment dropped from 72 out of every 1,000 jobs in the country in the early 1950s to 49 per 1,000 in 1972.

New York City has about 225,000 employing institutions, including businesses, nonprofit organizations, and governments. The typical firm employs relatively few people, however, only about 16 on the average, and this figure would be further reduced if the city's major public employers—the federal, state and city governments—were excluded from the data base.[42] Despite the small size of employment per firm and the heavy concentration of small family-owned and -operated enterprises, New York City remains the nation's key location for corporate headquarters. In 1971, of the United States' 500 largest industrial corporations, 119 were housed in New York City. This figure represents a net decline of about 9 percent, however, since 1960. Thus, employment in the administrative offices of manufacturing companies located in New York City dropped by almost 14 percent in the last ten years, while increasing by about 85 percent in the suburbs of New York.

The urban economy of New York City thus provides a substantial number of financial, producer, and government services, considerable wholesale and retail trade, and relatively little manufacturing, especially of durable goods. This industrial mix translates into an occupational structure in which white-collar jobs, especially professional, technical, and clerical types, play a prominent role (Table 1.5). More than one-quarter of the city's employed labor force occupies clerical positions, while almost another fourth consists of professional and technical workers, managers, proprietors, and officials.

TABLE 1.4

Leading Industries of Job Change, New York City, 1959-72

Industry	Number of Jobs in 1972	Change from 1959		Change from 1969	
		Number	Percent	Number	Percent
Industries of job growth					
Local government	423,800	157,900	59.4	20,500	5.1
Miscellaneous business services	183,400	68,500	59.6	- 15,400	- 7.7
Securities brokers, exchanges, and services	87,900	58,800	202.1	- 17,300	-16.4
Medical and other health services	164,400	49,800	43.5	23,100	16.3
Banking	129,400	41,400	47.0	4,500	3.6
Education (nongovernment)	76,500	29,800	63.8	- 300	- 0.4
Miscellaneous services	58,900	17,000	40.6	3,500	6.3
Nonprofit membership organizations	98,100	21,400	27.9	- 1,300	- 1.3
State government	41,200	15,000	57.3	3,000	7.9
Communications	89,200	12,800	16.8	3,100	3.6
Total	1,352,800	472,400	53.7	23,400	1.8
Industries of job decline					
Apparel manufacturing	186,500	- 91,900	- 33.0	- 37,000	-16.6
Water transportation	32,400	- 38,400	- 54.2	- 16,900	-34.3
Food and kindred products	47,400	- 34,700	- 42.3	- 13,900	-22.7
Real estate	95,600	- 13,300	- 12.2	2,600	2.8
Railroads	74,400	- 10,600	- 12.5	900	- 1.2
Fabricated metal products	31,300	- 15,500	- 33.0	- 6,100	-16.3
Federal government	98,500	- 15,200	- 13.4	- 7,000	- 6.6
Miscellaneous manufacturing industries	55,300	- 21,000	- 27.5	- 13,200	-19.3
Electrical machinery	39,700	- 17,600	- 30.7	- 10,100	-20.3
Machinery (except electrical)	20,900	- 13,700	- 39.6	- 7,300	-25.9
Total	682,000	-271,900	- 28.5	-113,200	-14.2

Sources: Compiled from source cited for Table 1.1 and from U.S. Department of Labor, Bureau of Labor Statistics, Middle Atlantic Regional Office, *New York City in Transition: Population, Jobs, Prices and Pay in a Decade of Change*, Regional Report No. 34, (Washington, D.C.: Government Printing Office, July 1973), p. 36.

TABLE 1.5

Occupational Distribution of
Employed, New York City, 1970

Occupational Group	Percent
Total	100.0
White-collar workers	57.9
Professional and technical	15.7
Managers, officials and proprietors	7.8
Clerical workers	27.1
Sales workers	7.3
Blue-collar workers	28.5
Craftsmen and foremen	10.2
All others*	18.3
Service workers	13.6
Private household	1.3
Other service workers	12.3

*Includes operatives, laborers, farm managers, and laborers. Farm managers and laborers comprise less than 1 percent of the total.

Sources: Compiled from source listed in Table 1.1, and U.S. Department of Labor, Bureau of Labor Statistics, Middle Atlantic Regional Office, *New York City in Transition: Population, Jobs, Prices and Pay in a Decade of Change*, Regional Report Number 34 (Washington, D.C.: Government Printing Office, July, 1973), p. 18.

Fewer than three out of ten wage and salary workers in New York City are in blue collar jobs, with another 13.5 percent occupying service positions. Nationally, by contrast, nearly 50 percent of the U.S. workforce is in blue-collar and service jobs.

Population and Labor Force Characteristics

The composition of New York City's population changed markedly in recent years even as total population increased only slightly. In 1970, for example, persons 15-24 years old accounted for about 16 percent of the city's population; those 65 years old and older, for 12 percent. Ten years earlier the corresponding percentages were 12.5 and 10.5 percent respectively. In 1950, of the city's residents, 87 percent were white, 10 percent

"Negro and other races," and 3 percent Puerto Rican. By 1970 the proportion of whites among the 7,895,000 New Yorkers declined to 67 percent, while the categories "Negro and other races" and Puerto Ricans increased to 23 and 10 percent respectively. Indeed, between 1960 and 1970, the rate of population increase among "Negro and other races" in New York City surpassed those of all other major U.S. cities, due in large part to net immigration.

Minority group members of New York City's labor force have made important occupational employment gains in recent years (Table 1.6). By 1970, 43 percent of employed black New Yorkers and 33.5 percent of the city's Puerto Rican workers were in white-collar occupations, up from 29 and 19 percent respectively in 1960. Approximately 10 percent of the city's black workers held professional and technical jobs in 1970, as compared with less than 7 percent in 1960, with female blacks having relatively greater representation than men (12.2 versus 7.9 percent). Importantly, the proportion of black females employed as private household workers declined from 21 percent in 1960 to about 9 percent in 1970. Relative to the total New York City work force, however, minority employees are overrepresented in blue-collar and service occupations.

Long-term occupational gains constitute only one part—in some ways a small part—of the labor market experiences of New York City's ethnic minorities. For example, in the city's "high unemployment" neighborhoods (neighborhoods in which unemployment rates are at least double that of the city as a whole), 46 percent of the population is black, 24 percent Puerto Rican. In these neighborhoods, labor force participation rates are substantially lower than in the rest of the city; three of every five employed people are in blue-collar and service jobs, compared with two of five in the rest of the city; median family income is about 27 percent lower than that reported for the entire city in 1970; and almost one of every five 16- to 21-year-old males is not enrolled in school, is not a high school graduate, is unemployed or not in the labor force, compared with only one in ten throughout New York City. Further, whereas 15 percent of the city's population had incomes below the poverty level in 1969, 24 percent of the city's blacks and 35 percent of its Puerto Ricans were living in poverty during the same year. Finally, in contrast to the rest of the nation, the proportion of families with income below the poverty level in New York City diminished hardly at all over the ten-year period ending in 1969.

Pay and Price Trends

Despite the recent decline in aggregate employment and rise in unemployment, New York City earnings levels have increased at relatively high rates in the last several years. However, consideration of the rapid pace of price changes in New York City leads to considerably lower estimates of the "real" earnings gains of the city's wage and salary workforce.

15

TABLE 1.6

Occupational Distribution of Employed, by Ethnic Group, New York City, 1960 and 1970[a]

Occupational Group	Total		Black[b]		Puerto Rican[c]	
	1960	1970	1960	1970	1960	1970
Total						
White-collar workers	51.7	57.9	29.2	43.1	18.7	33.4
Professional and technical	12.0	15.7	6.8	9.9	2.4	4.8
Managers, officials, and proprietors	9.4	7.8	3.4	3.1	2.8	3.6
Clerical workers	22.8	27.1	16.2	26.7	10.6	20.2
Sales workers	7.5	7.3	2.8	3.4	2.9	4.8
Blue-collar workers	35.2	28.5	40.8	32.9	65.1	48.1
Craftsmen and foremen	11.1	10.2	7.0	9.0	8.0	11.3
All others[d]	24.1	18.3	33.8	23.9	57.1	36.8
Service workers	13.0	13.6	29.9	24.0	16.1	18.5
Private household	2.1	1.3	9.8	4.5	.3	.3
Other service workers	10.9	12.3	20.1	19.5	15.8	18.2
Men						
White-collar workers	45.9	49.2	27.0	33.3	18.2	27.2
Professional and technical	11.8	15.4	5.2	7.9	2.2	4.0
Managers, officials, and proprietors	12.4	10.6	5.0	4.3	3.7	4.5
Clerical workers	13.4	14.8	14.1	17.2	9.2	13.7
Sales workers	8.3	8.4	2.7	3.9	3.1	5.0
Blue-collar workers	42.4	37.7	50.9	47.5	61.3	51.6
Craftsmen and foremen	16.6	16.2	11.6	15.3	11.2	15.5
All others[d]	25.8	21.5	39.3	32.2	50.1	36.1
Service workers	11.7	13.1	22.0	19.2	20.6	21.2
Private household	.2	.1	.9	.3	.1	.1
Other service workers	11.5	13.0	21.1	18.9	20.5	21.1

(Continued)

Occupational Group	Total		Black[b]		Puerto Rican[c]	
	1960	1970	1960	1970	1960	1970
Women						
White-collar workers	62.2	70.9	32.0	54.7	19.9	46.5
Professional and technical	12.3	16.3	8.8	12.2	2.9	6.5
Managers, officials, and proprietors	4.1	3.8	1.4	1.8	1.1	1.7
Clerical workers	39.6	45.1	18.9	37.8	13.4	34.0
Sales workers	6.2	5.7	2.9	2.9	2.5	4.3
Blue-collar workers	22.5	15.1	27.9	15.7	72.4	40.6
Craftsmen and foremen	1.4	1.4	1.2	1.5	1.9	2.4
All others[d]	21.1	13.7	26.7	14.2	70.5	38.2
Service workers	15.3	14.0	40.0	29.6	7.7	12.9
Private household	5.5	2.9	21.2	9.4	.8	.8
Other service workers	9.8	11.1	18.8	20.2	6.9	12.1

[a]1960 data are for employed persons age 14 and over; 1970 data are for employed persons age 16 and over. The effect of the 1970 exclusion of 14 and 15 year olds is minimal; in 1970 there were 13,152 employed persons 14 and 15 years old, or 0.4 percent of all employed persons.

[b]1960 data include "Negroes and other races." In 1960, blacks comprised 95.3 percent of the category, "Negroes and other races."

[c]Puerto Rican data are for the New York area (New York City, Nassau-Suffolk, Westchester, and Rockland Counties). In 1970, 96 percent of all Puerto Ricans in the New York area lived in New York City; in 1960, 97 percent lived in the city.

[d]Includes operatives, laborers, and farm managers and laborers. Farm managers and laborers comprised less than 1 percent of the total in both 1960 and 1970 and have no significant impact on the data.

Sources: Compiled from source cited for Table 1.1 and from U.S. Department of Labor, Bureau of Labor Statistics, Middle Atlantic Regional Office, *New York City in Transition: Population, Jobs, Prices and Pay in a Decade of Change,* Regional Report No. 34, (Washington, D.C.: Government Printing Office, July 1973), p. 18.

Table 1.7 presents earnings data for a group of occupations for which the U.S. Bureau of Labor Statistics conducts annual wage surveys. Clearly, for the years shown, the (nominal) earnings gains of New York City workers exceeded those of workers employed throughout the United States. When adjusted for differences in the cost of living, however, the relative wage advantage of New York City workers is reversed in all but one of the occupations listed ("unskilled plant"). Analysis of *real* earnings increases for a group of professional occupations—accountants, auditors, attorneys, and engineers—yielded similar results. Thus, whereas New York City is in some ways and for some occupations a high wage area, it is certainly (and more emphatically) a high-price area. As a consequence, the "attractiveness of New York City as a labor market ... may be diminishing, especially for ... professional and skilled workers."[43]

Having explicated some relevant dimensions of the New York City labor market, we introduce the individual studies that form the substance of this book.

TABLE 1.7

Percent Increases in Earnings and Consumer Prices, United States and New York City, 1969-72

Industry and Occupation	United States	New York Area	New York City
Earnings			
Office clerical	19.7	22.6	22.5
Skilled maintenance	22.7	23.3	25.9
Unskilled plant	23.9	27.9	30.8
Factory production	19.2	22.0	21.4
Consumer Prices	15.6	18.9	18.9
"Real Earnings"			
Office clerical	3.5	3.1	3.0
Skilled maintenance	6.1	3.7	5.9
Unskilled plant	7.2	7.6	10.0
Factory production	3.1	2.6	2.1

Sources: Compiled from source cited for Table 1.1 and from U.S. Department of Labor, Bureau of Labor Statistics, Middle Atlantic Regional Office, *New York City in Transition: Population, Jobs, Prices and Pay in a Decade of Change,* Regional Report No. 34, (Washington, D.C.: Government Printing Office, July 1973), p. 57.

Our first study examines labor market information as it affects a group of individuals who occupy marginal positions in society and thus "peripheral" status in the labor force: criminal offenders. Most societies handle offenders by making many of them prisoners—a process not unlike the conversion of the mentally ill into patients. This is done by means of institutionalization, whereby the "deviant" is removed from the larger society. Except for the most severe cases, however, institutionalization is not considered a permanent condition. Most offenders are expected to return to society (and they do), though they may well recidivate at relatively high rates. Consequently, it seems important to explore the process by which the formerly institutionalized return to society and, relatedly, the role of labor market information in this process.

In recent years, some U.S. manpower programs have been directed specifically towards criminal offenders.[44] However, these programs tend to have a static human capital orientation. That is, they assume that the provision of a lumpy investment (for example, in vocational training, remedial education, or supportive services) to the offender increases that individual's quality and thus his salability in the labor market. These programs, which have proliferated and grown more diverse as a result of contemporary federal legislation, are reviewed in Chapter 2.

More fundamental to our analysis, however, are the conceptual underpinnings of current manpower programs for the institutionalized. We take issue with the static conception of these programs, which ignores the *process* of institutionalization, and argue instead for a dynamic or flow concept of institutionalization. Succinctly stated, elements of the flow process include pre-incarcerative employment experiences, attitudes, and demographic factors; the institutional experience, including exposure to manpower programs where available, but also to the variety of other experiences uniquely characteristic of the "total" institutions;[45] the functioning of labor markets, especially the local urban market, and the manner in which labor market information is transmitted through intermediaries or by other means to the formerly institutionalized individual; employer-personnel practices, notably hiring and selection practices and, relatedly, the degree of labor market tightness; and, finally, the labor market experiences of the formerly institutionalized during the post-release period. The flow model implies that manipulation of any single variable or set of variables (for example, vocational training) in connection with the institutionalized may be expected to facilitate only marginally the individual's return to society and integration with the labor force.

Proceeding from this dynamic model, we examine the role and uses of labor market information for ex-offenders who encounter the urban labor market operative in New York City. Two critical factors are specifically considered: (a) the role of intermediaries in the labor market experiences of the formerly institutionalized and (b) the system of inmate manpower utilization predominant in correctional institutions.

In their labor market information model, Yavitz and Morse point to the critical role occupied by intermediaries "whose actions significantly modify the flows and arrivals of the two main inputs into the job market."[46] For conventional labor force participants, intermediaries impacting directly on the market include friends and relatives, employment agencies, and data banks. For the formerly institutionalized, however, relevant intermediaries may include the probation officer, the parole officer, the "therapeutic community," and the so-called halfway house (in addition to the correctional institution itself). In Chapter 3, we examine the ways in which these intermediaries acquire and transmit labor market information to ex-offenders in New York City and, consequently, how intermediaries affect the labor market experiences of this group. The intermediary is viewed essentially as a surrogate for the formerly institutionalized person in the labor market, bearing the costs of job search, information acquisition, and job development.

Our concern with the system of inmate manpower utilization in the prison stems from recognition of the divergence of this system from systems of manpower utilization in more conventional worlds of work and, relatedly, the implications of this divergence for labor market information and its utilization in the urban setting. In other words, these institutions develop and are characterized by secondary labor market behavior.[47] Specifically, in correctional institutions, authority flows principally from the top down; supervision is close and unilateral; due process (for example, via appeals procedures) is rarely given formal consideration. In the "outside" world, authority is relatively more diffuse, flowing from diverse sources and through multiple channels; supervision is less unilateral and frequently bargainable; systems of due process characterize both union and nonunion situations. The work undertaken by (or required of) inmates of correctional institutions is most often of an unskilled or semiskilled nature, performed on an irregular or attenuated basis, and rewarded (if at all) by abysmally low rates of compensation. On the outside, in contrast, job skills are both more diverse and typically of a higher order; work shifts and work patterns are more stable; compensation is much higher, more regular, and paid in wages rather than in kind. The technology and pattern of factor utilization in correctional institutions is typically stagnant and the capital-labor ratio low, reminding one of the economies of less-developed countries. In sum, the system of inmate manpower utilization in prisons is not linked to dynamic product (or labor) markets where changes in work patterns and work methods continually occur and where accepted conventions of the workaday world obtain. Because both intermediaries, who provide labor market information, and the formerly institutionalized, who are exposed to information, must deal with the peculiar effects of the institutionalization process, the system of manpower utilization in correctional institutions is a central concern of this study.

The second study in this book, presented in Chapters 4 and 5, is concerned with labor market information and the educational system. The output of this system is the primary source of newly-trained entrants to the labor market. While in the case of an urban economy local educational institutions cannot supply all of the trained manpower required (especially in high-skilled and professional occupations), they do significantly affect the skill level of those persons available for employment for the first time. This is particularly true of New York City, which has a well-established, diversified, and integrated network of educational institutions. The main concern here, then, is how and to what extent labor market information influences the decisions of educational planners and administrators in the setting of enrollment levels and in curriculum selection. New York's public secondary vocational high schools and two- and four-year public colleges were chosen for examination as they train for multiple occupations and comprise a major portion of the city's educational system. To the extent that these schools base their decisions on (and adequately interpret) labor market information, an improved match between the skills taught and those demanded in the labor market should ensue.

The selection of a curriculum and the specific skills to be taught in educational institutions has not always been considered an important dimension of the educational planning process. A large majority of occupations in the economy were at one time unskilled, and others did not require pre-employment training as this was frequently provided on the job. This situation changed, however, with the growth of the technological and service economy, which emphasized increased utilization of skilled manpower and the development of new occupational specialties. The New York City economy and labor force reflected these changes in their industrial and occupational structures respectively. As noted earlier, the leading sectors of the city's employment growth during the 1960s were those requiring relatively high skilled labor (local government, finance, and medical, educational, and business services) while industries registering the largest declines (apparel and food manufacturing) had relatively low skill requirements. Concomitantly, the occupations characteristic of New York City's resident labor force were increasingly the professional, technical, and clerical types. The only occupational category experiencing a significant decline during this period was that of operatives.[48]

By expanding its training capabilities, the educational system played a major role in meeting the skill demands of U.S. labor markets, including New York City's, in this economic dynamic. There was increased enrollment in two- and four-year public and private colleges, a new and enlarged program of secondary and adult public vocational education, the creation of government-sponsored manpower training programs, and the growth of proprietary post-secondary training institutions. In general, these programs expanded at a faster rate than the economy. For example, on a national basis, expenditures for public and private higher education rose from $2.1 to $24.9 billion between 1950 and 1970, or from 0.8 to 2.7 percent of the gross national product.[49] Expecting further increases in the skill demands of the economy and continued growth of the education sector, increased emphasis has been placed on the utilization of labor market information to improve the match between the demand and supply of trained manpower.

Whether labor market information can perform this matching function depends upon the interactions of the three centers of activity: (a) the individual student engaged in the educational system, (b) the working mechanisms of the labor market, and (c) the planning and operating process of the educational institution. In the systems view of the labor market offered by Yavitz and Morse, primary and secondary schools, institutions of higher education, and

21

vocational and specific-skill training comprise several of the components of a manpower development subsystem.[50] The schools act as service organizations to the individual student directly and to the employment subsystem indirectly through the labor market. Therefore, the determination of enrollments and areas of instruction is viewed as influenced by the preferences of students on the one hand, and by the conditions in the labor market on the other. In addition, each educational institution is confronted by an internal set of constraints that include administrative procedures, finances, (materials and) equipment, and faculty. The way information about the structure of, access to, and general conditions in the labor market is currently evaluated, interpreted, and used by educational planners and administrators to shape curriculum and determine enrollments within the limits of internal operational factors and student influence is the subject of this investigation.

The third study, presented in Chapters 6 and 7, focuses on labor market information and the three major intermediaries in the local labor market—employers, unions, and municipal government. The decisions of these actors (along with the decisions of some other actors—for example, the federal government—not explicitly considered here) are instrumental in defining the local labor market. In the course of reaching their individual and collective decisions, these intermediaries rely heavily on labor market information; but they are also influenced mightily by decision-making considerations that have little to do with information.

The central focus of the third study is on the government of New York City. In New York, however, as in most other large U.S. cities, local government stands in close relation to organized business and labor interests. This does not mean that the primary interests of the three major groups are always compatible. Depending on the issue, this triad of major actors might relate with one another cooperatively, antagonistically, or not at all. The extent to which the informational component plays a role in their decisional interactions is often dependent on the compatibility of their interests.

The most striking feature of New York City is its complexity. No other U.S. city is so large or diverse. The city's labor market and each of the major intermediaries examined in this study reflect the characteristics of the larger social system. The question, whether New York City's size and diversity make it unique, is not answered in this study; however, the effect of the city's complexity on the role and potential of labor market information is centrally considered.

To date, most theories or models of labor market information have been cast in relatively simple settings—for example, the prospective employer-prospective employee relationships. Large, pluralistic social systems generally feature, among other things, however, pronounced conflict among major actors or groups. Many obstacles pertaining to the acquisition, transmission, interpretation, and ultimate utility of labor market information exist in a pluralistic city such as New York, and on a scale not found in smaller, more homogeneous communities. While the benefits to be realized from an improved information system in a large city would perhaps far exceed those in a small city, it also would seem that realizing those benefits will be far more difficult in the former than in the latter.

22

It is now widely understood that urban economies and labor markets are not moved to full and efficient performance by simple (even substantial) increases in aggregate or national demand. It is also widely understood that improving the supply of labor through local initiatives, such as education and manpower training programs, is extremely difficult, particularly in an economy such as New York's, which is not generating an increased number of jobs and which has experienced substantial alteration in the composition of its occupational structure.

An improved local labor market information system is not desirable in and of itself but rather because, assumedly, it would affect (though indirectly) both the demand and supply sides of the local economy. Improved labor market information must be viewed as an instrumental tool that can provide assistance not only to governmental actors oriented toward improving the quality of the local labor supply but also to employers and unions interested in increasing the level of local economic activity.

The purpose of local labor market information and the rationale for improving it are independent of any set of local structural or endogenous characteristics. All urban labor markets would no doubt reap some benefits from having their major employing institutions, union organizations, and local government possessed of better information about the local economy. The third study, then, focuses on the impact of structural characteristics in one large urban economy, that of New York City, on the character of existing labor market information, its utilization, and the prospects for its improvement.

In the final chapter of this book we offer a set of recommendations intended to aid those charged with the thorny task of designing public manpower policies, especially policies that pertain to labor market information. These recommendations flow from the major findings of each of the studies presented here and, as such, differ from each other in scope and emphasis. Further, whereas some recommendations are quite compatible with the assumptions underlying current policies and programs regarding labor market information, others provide challenges to these assumptions. This occurs not out of a desire to seek change for the sake of change or out of any vested interest in alternative policies, but, instead, to let policy be informed by knowledge of the uses and limits of manpower information in the metropolis.

NOTES

1. Allan M. Cartter and F. Ray Marshall, *Labor Economics: Wages, Employment, and Trade Unionism*, Rev. ed. (Homewood, Ill.: Irwin, 1972), p. 162.

2. Lloyd G. Reynolds, *Labor Economics and Labor Relations* (Englewood Cliffs, N.J.: Prentice-Hall, 1970), p. 79.

3. Ibid., p. 97. Reynolds labels these "equalizing" differentials—that is, "differences required to equalize the net advantages of various occupations to workers on the margin of decision."

4. Adam Smith, *The Wealth of Nations* (New York: Modern Library, 1937), pp. 100-7.

5. Reynolds, op. cit., pp. 87-88.

6. George J. Stigler, "Information in the Labor Market," *Journal of Political Economy*, 70 (Supplement: October 1962): 94-95.

7. Ibid., p. 94.

8. Ibid., pp. 97-103. For a recent empirical test of the wage-search substitution hypothesis, see Albert Rees and George P. Schultz, *Workers and Wages in an Urban Labor Market* (Chicago: University of Chicago Press, 1972), Ch. 12.

9. Armen A. Alchian, "Information Costs, Pricing, and Resource Unemployment," in *Microeconomic Foundations of Employment and Inflation Theory*, E. S. Phelps et al., eds. (New York: Norton, 1970), p. 27.

10. Ibid., p. 28.

11. Ibid.

12. Charles C. Holt, "Job Search, Phillips' Wage Relation and Union Influence: Theory and Evidence," in Phelps et al., eds., op. cit., pp. 53-123, esp. 53-74.

13. Charles C. Holt, "Improving the Labor Market Tradeoff between Inflation and Unemployment," *American Economic Review: Papers and Proceedings of the Eighty-First Annual Meeting*, 59, no. 2 (May, 1969): 135-46; Charles C. Holt, "How Can the Phillips' Curve Be Moved to Reduce Both Inflation and Unemployment?" in Phelps et al., eds., op. cit., pp. 224-56; Charles C. Holt et al., *The Unemployment-Inflation Dilemma: A Manpower Solution* (Washington, D.C.: The Urban Institute, 1971). Holt et al. actually offer a variety of manpower proposals, including some pertaining to training and job restructuring, geographic mobility, and employment opportunities for youth. In the present discussion, we concentrate on the information-related recommendations of these authors.

14. Holt, "Job Search, Phillips' Wage Relation, and Union Influence: ...."; Holt et al., op. cit.; A. W. Phillips, "The Relation between Unemployment and the Rate of Change of Money Wage Rates in the United Kingdom, 1861-1957," *Economica*, 25 (November 1958): 283-99. Holt and his colleagues do, of course, recognize the distinction between short-run and long-run relationships between unemployment and inflation in formulating their policy recommendations.

15. Edmund S. Phelps, "Money Wage Dynamics and Labor Market Equilibrium," in Phelps et al., eds., op. cit., pp. 124-66; Milton Friedman, "The Role of Monetary Policy," *American Economic Review*, 58 (March 1968): 1-17; Samuel Morley, *The Economics of Inflation* (Hinsdale, Ill.: Dryden Press, 1971), Chs. 1, 3, 5, 6.

16. Morely, op. cit., Ch. 6.

17. See, for example, Charles C. Killingsworth, "The Continuing Labor Market Twist," *Monthly Labor Review*, 91 (September, 1958): 12-17.

18. Boris Yavitz and Dean W. Morse, *The Labor Market: An Information System* (New York: Praeger, 1973), p. 78.

19. Ibid., p. 82.

20. Ibid., p. 115. Note the detailed discussion on pp. 95-114.

21. Ibid.

22. For example, the illegal labor market offers considerable incentives to residents of urban areas, especially the inner city. See Stanley L. Friedlander and Robert Schick, *Unemployment in the Urban Core* (New York: Praeger, 1972), pp. 113-14, 173-82, 184-89. They estimate that in 1966, 33 percent of Harlem's residents classified as not in the labor force derived their income from illegal sources and, further, that the portion deriving at least part of their income illegally may be even larger among part-time and full-time workers residing in Harlem. The minimum amount of illegal income obtained by Harlem residents is estimated by Friedlander and Schick to be $150 million in 1966. Ibid., pp. 186-89.

23. Charles C. Holt et al., "Manpower Proposals for Phase Three," *Brookings Paper on Economic Activity*, no. 3 (Washington, D.C.: The Brookings Institution, 1971), pp. 703-22.

24. See, for example, Charles C. Holt and G. P. Gruber, "A Computer-Aided Approach to Employment Service, Placement, and Counseling," *Management Science*, 15 (July 1969): 573-94.

25. U.S. Department of Labor, "Job Bank and Job Matching," in U.S. President, *Manpower Report of the President—1970* (Washington, D.C.: Government Printing Office, 1970), pp. 199-205.

26. William Haber and Daniel H. Kruger, *The Role of the United States Employment Service in a Changing Economy* (Kalamazoo, Mich.: The W. E. Upjohn Institute for Employment Research, 1964); Stanley H. Ruttenburg and Jocelyn Gutchess, *The Federal-State Employment Service: A Critique* (Baltimore: The Johns Hopkins Press, 1970).

27. Eli Ginzberg, "Foreword," in Yavitz and Morse, op. cit., p. x.

28. See George P. Huber and Joseph C. Ullman, *A Study of the Local Job Bank Program: Performance, Structure, and Direction*, reported in U.S. Department of Labor, Manpower Administration, "Summaries of R & D Reports, No. 9" (Washington, D.C.: Office of Research and Development, December 1972). Contrary to popular assumption, the introduction of computer technology in local ES offices may not improve either the functioning or services of this agency.

29. See Rees and Shultz, op. cit., pp. 199-207; F. Theodore Malm, "Recruiting Patterns and the Functioning of Labor Markets," in *Management of Human Resources*, F. Theodore Malm, Paul Pigors, and Charles A. Myers, eds. (New York: McGraw-Hill, 1964), pp. 242-56; David Lewin, "The Employer Probe: Employer Utilization of Labor Market Information," in Yavitz and Morse, pp. 63-72.

30. Also see Albert Rees, "Information Networks in Labor Markets," *American Economic Review: Papers and Proceedings of the Seventy-Eighth Annual Meeting* (May 1966): 559-66.

31. Ibid., p. 561.

32. Yavitz and Morse, op. cit., p. 147.

33. See Subcommittee on Employment, Manpower, and Poverty of the Committee on Labor and Public Welfare, United States Senate, *The Emergency Employment Act: An Interim Assessment* (Washington, D.C.: Government Printing Office, May 1972), esp. pp. 5-8.

34. Daniel S. Hammermesh, *Economic Aspects of Manpower Training Programs* (Lexington, Mass.: Heath, 1971), esp. pp. 1-42.

35. Ibid., pp. 122-27.

36. Ibid., pp. 119-22. As Holt does, Hammermesh argues that "improving the short-run trade-off between inflation and unemployment should also be the central goal for manpower training in the United States" (p. 121).

37. Yavitz and Morse, op. cit., p. 302.

38. Unless otherwise indicated all data in this section are from U.S. Department of Labor, Bureau of Labor Statistics, Middle Atlantic Regional Office, *New York City in Transition: Population, Jobs, Prices and Pay in a Decade of Change*, Regional Report No. 34 (Washington, D.C.: Government Printing Office, July 1973).

39. U.S. Department of Commerce, Bureau of the Census, *Statistical Abstract of the United States—1971* (Washington, D.C.: Government Printing Office, 1972), pp. 844, 864.

40. U.S. Department of Labor, Bureau of Labor Statistics, Middle Atlantic Regional Office, *1972 Year-End Report on Employment, Prices, and Earnings in New York City*, Regional Report No. 33 (Washington, D.C.: Government Printing Office, December 1972), p. 2.

41. This is the theme emphasized in *New York Is Very Much Alive*, Eli Ginzbert et al., eds. (New York: McGraw-Hill, 1973), notably the "Foreword," pp. xi-xv, and Ch. 16, pp. 285-96.

42. Computed from data in New York State Department of Commerce, *New York State Business Fact Book, Part I* (1972).

43. U.S. Department of Labor, *New York City in Transition*, pp. 63-64.

44. See Robert Taggart III, *The Prison of Unemployment: Manpower Programs for Offenders* (Baltimore: The Johns Hopkins Press, 1972), pp. 25-49. Section 251 of the Manpower Development and Training Act, added in 1966, authorized experimental and demonstration manpower projects for prison inmates.

45. See Erving Goffman, "The Characteristics of Total Institutions," in *A Sociological Reader on Complex Organizations*, 2d ed., Amitai Etzioni, ed. (New York: Holt, Rinehart and Winston, 1969), pp. 312-38; Theodore Caplow, *Principles of Organization* (New York: Harcourt, Brace and World, 1964), pp. 169-200. Correctional institutions are, of course, only one among several types of "total" institutions in society, all of which differ markedly from other institutional forms.

46. Yavitz and Morse, op. cit., p. 115.

47. See Michael J. Piore, "On the Job Training in the Dual Labor Market," *Public-Private Manpower Policies*, Arnold R. Weber et al., eds. (Madison, Wis.: IRRA, 1969), pp. 101-32; Piore, *Notes for a Theory of Labor Market Stratification*, working paper, Department of Economics, no. 95 (MIT, October 1972).

48. "U.S. Census of Population and Housing 1960, Final Report PHC (1)-104, Census Tracts New York, N.Y." (Washington, D.C.: U.S. Department of Commerce, 1962), Table P-3, p. 517; "1970 Census of Population, PC(1)-C34, General Economic and Social Characteristics, New York" (Washington, D.C.: U.S. Department of Commerce, 1972), Table 86, pp. 343-72.

49. *Statistical Abstract of the United States 1971* (Washington, D.C.: U.S. Department of Commerce, 1971), Table 150, p. 102.

50. Yavitz and Morse, op. cit., Ch. 2.

CHAPTER

2

MANPOWER SERVICES
FOR OFFENDERS:
THE INSTITUTIONAL
DYNAMIC

In the United States, there are approximately 400,000 persons in correctional institutions—that is, federal and state prisons, juvenile detention centers, and local jails (see Table 2.1).[1] Each year, however, a substantial number of individuals flow into and out of these institutions. (For example, although the population of federal and state prisons increased by only .2 of 1 percent between January 1 and December 31, 1970, almost 256,000 prisoners were admitted during the year and almost 254,000 discharges were recorded.[2] In 1967 the President's Commission on Law Enforcement and the Administration of Justice estimated that on any given day the corrections system in the United States is responsible for approximately 1.3 million offenders.) Upon release, former prisoners are not only expected to return to society but also to maintain themselves to such a degree that they need not return to a correctional facility (that is, recidivate). Obviously, a major determinant of the post-institutional experience is employment or, more accurately, access to employment. In this context, it becomes important to explore the role of labor market information in facilitating employment and the process by which the formerly institutionalized return to society.

In the present chapter we will examine recent manpower programs, including some centered in New York City, directed at U.S. offenders. Noting the limited impact of these programs, we will then develop a flow model of institutionalization, explicating its labor market implications. This model leads, in Chapter 3, to an investigation of labor market behavior among former prisoners in New York City. The analysis focuses particularly on labor market intermediaries for the formerly institutionalized and on the system of manpower utilization in total institutions as it affects subsequent labor market behavior. Finally, policy recommendations stemming from this investigation are adumbrated in Chapter 8.

TABLE 2.1

Inmates of Correctional and Delinquency Institutions, United States and New York State, 1970

Level of Institution	United States	New York State
Federal Prisons	20,038	—
State Prisions	176,391	12,059*
Local Jails	160,863	17,399
Subtotals	357,292	29,458
Institutions for delinquent children		
State	44,518	2,773
Local	5,293	—
Subtotals	49,811	2,773
Total	407,103	32,231

*Federal and state combined.

Sources: U.S. Bureau of the Census, *The Statistical Abstract of the U.S.* (Washington, D.C.: Government Printing Office, 1973), pp. 160-61; U.S. Department of Justice, Law Enforcement Assistance Administration, *1970 National Jail Census* (Washington, D.C.: LEAA, February 1971), pp. 2, 9; U.S. Department of Health, Education and Welfare, *Statistics on Public Institutions for Delinquent Children, 1970* (Washington, D.C.: National Center for Social Statistics, June 30, 1971), pp. 3, 10.

MANPOWER SERVICES FOR THE INSTITUTIONALIZED

Because, in theory, prisons seek to rehabilitate their inmates, some manpower services (for example, education and training) have long been provided by these institutions. Such efforts, however, are generally unsystematic, are confined to a small proportion of inmate populations, and have only a limited impact upon recipients. Thus, in a large-scale study of federal prisoners released during the mid-1960s, Pownall found that "vocational training . . . programs . . . are concentrated primarily in the youth institutions. These programs have little effect on released prisoners as indicated by the negligible differences in employment rates between those who did and those who did not have vocational training."[3]

Under the Manpower Development and Training Act of 1962 (MDTA) several experimental and demonstration programs were conceived to further explore the effectiveness of vocational training as well as remedial education

29

and selected supportive services. Considerable success was claimed for these programs, and in 1966 Congress amended section 251 to MDTA, authorizing the secretary of labor to substantially expand prison projects.

Interestingly, the Rikers Island Project, conducted between 1963 and 1965 in New York City,[4] was widely cited as an example of a "successful" prison program and consequently played a large role in the expansion of MDTA. This project involved training in keypunch operations, remedial reading, counseling, job placement assistance, and a cash payment upon release for 137 16-to-21-year-old males. When compared with a control group of 127 men who received no special aids or training, the "experimentals," including drug addicts, recidivated at lower rates and achieved better jobs. However, the experimental and control groups differed significantly in terms of the proportion of drug users and the extent of addiction among actual users. These factors had an important impact on variation in post-release employment experiences. Further:

> ... only 29 percent of the experimental group were hired for work even indirectly related to their ... training and only 18 percent specifically for such jobs. Placement was difficult in keypunch jobs because employers did not want to have offenders working next to women, who predominate in this occupation. ... [The] experimental group's greater penetration of white-collar jobs was largely the result of placement efforts rather than vocational training per se.[5]

These findings (which, incidentally, point up the lack of attention paid to local labor market information), together with the unusual leadership provided in the Rikers Island Program and the more general problem of replicating experimental—small—projects on a large scale, call into question the basis for (though not the intent of) the aforementioned expansion of MDTA.

What has been the general experience with prison programs recently supported by U.S. manpower policy—the so-called 251 projects? Some findings are provided in a study of the labor market experiences of about 2,500 released offenders who were enrolled in 25 of these programs.[6] When compared with a control group of 1,100 individuals, trainees experienced (a) a small but statistically significant reduction in recidivism; (b) no significant differences in post-release performance as measured by employment status, hourly wage, percent of time employed, and total earnings; (c) no significant differences in the effects of personal characteristics on recidivism or employment, and (d) no significant differences in the effects of such institutional variables as counseling, vocational training, basic education, trainee selection methods, job development and placement, and costs on either recidivism or employment experience.

Because the evaluation cited above purports to be the most comprehensive yet conducted of prison manpower programs, it is important to recognize, if only briefly, its conceptual and methodological limitations. First, little or no attention is given to the theoretical underpinnings of these programs or to the manpower policies from which they derive. More important, no consideration

30

is given to either labor market or sociological theory, both of which seem crucial to an understanding of attempts to use total institutions as vehicles for improving the employability of offenders. Second, owing to a required methodological adjustment, data analysis was actually performed on a sample about two-thirds smaller than originally specified. This may have increased representativeness (as the evaluators claim), but it also introduces some bias into the data and confounds portions of the statistical analysis. Third, no control groups were used in 9 of the 25 projects, thus creating problems of data interpretation and, indeed, scientific acceptability. Fourth, the effects of pre-incarceration labor market experiences, socioeconomic variables, and institutional characteristics on both recidivism and employment were discerned primarily through simple two-variable cross-tabulations. A multivariate analysis of the data, seemingly a necessity in this sort of evaluation, was not performed. Finally, the level of statistical significance used in interpreting the findings varies considerably throughout the study. Despite these weaknesses and the almost imperceptible impact of the projects on the employability of offenders, the authors of this investigation recommend that "the Department of Labor continue and expand its inmate training program!"[7]

Of course, one should not pretend that even the most competent research serves as the basis for the formation or development of public policy. As Mangum notes:

> For a researcher, there is some reluctance to admit how few of the manpower programs legislated during the 1960's had their base in research identifying either problems or solutions. . . . For the most part, manpower legislation emerged in response to the relatively unguided conceptions (or misconceptions) of policy-makers.[8]

Furthermore, once initiated, a program tends to have a life (and a constituency) of its own, and seeks out new publics to serve. Whereas MDTA originated out of a concern for the skilled worker displaced by technological change, tight labor markets and recognition of the automation "bogey" shifted the focus toward the disadvantaged minorities, the poor and the unskilled. The 1970-71 recession and recent reductions of military manpower have caused still further shifts in the target groups for MDTA.[9] Viewed in this light, the expansion of prison training programs under federal manpower policy is perhaps more easily understood.

It should not be assumed that vocational training is the sole or even primary type of manpower effort aimed at prison inmates. Education programs, for example, are the most frequently offered prison manpower service. In general, however, these programs have a low rate of inmate participation, use outmoded facilities and techniques, and have virtually no impact on participants. More recently, the Draper Project, conducted at Elmore, Alabama, apparently found that exposure to basic education has a positive impact upon an inmate's employability after release.[10] Those who achieved high school equivalency—that is, GED—had even more favorable labor market experiences. However, it was unclear whether and to what extent other variables—for example, pre-incarceration labor market experiences—affected

31

employment, and whether educational services by themselves could have an important effect on prison inmates, especially those subject to short-term incarceration.

It is sometimes overlooked that inmates perform a considerable amount of "work" in prison, although much of this work involves the maintenance of the institution. To the question, How do such activities affect employability after release? the apparent answer is, Hardly at all. Among a sample of former inmates of federal prisons, "institutional work assignment was not significantly related to employment status upon release."[1] Indeed, those inmates participating in federal prison industries were more likely to be unemployed than persons performing unskilled maintenance work. While, at first glance, it appears that those who worked in prison subsequently achieved greater labor market success than those who did not, analysis showed that the most handicapped and/or behaviorally inadequate persons were excluded from work assignments. In other words, methods of selection (and exclusion) determined the different labor market experiences among subgroups of released offenders. Finally, only one of every seven released offenders located a first job related to work in prison, and only one in five subsequently attained a training or experience-related position.

Recently, the concept of work-release has gained wide currency among supporters of prison manpower programs. By working outside the prison during the day and returning at night, an inmate presumably contributes to society, learns (or learns to appreciate) discipline, and has access to income out of which basic expenses can be met and perhaps savings achieved. However, work-release is not practiced on a large scale. In 1970 fewer than one in ten federal prisoners were involved in a program of work-release, and the proportion was even smaller at the local level.[12] Among the 25 projects with MDTA programs referred to previously, 60 percent had no work-release program, 32 percent had a minimum program serving at most 10 percent of the total population, and only 12 percent had as many as one in five of their inmates on work-release.[13] For the most part, work-release was provided to those with minimum security status, those with "clean records," and those who were near the end of their sentences. A follow-up study of work-release enrollees during 1967, conducted by the Federal Bureau of Prisons, seemed to show a significantly lower rate of recidivism than among nonenrollees.[14] Again though, prisoners with the cleanest records and lowest probability of recidivism were chosen for participation in the program. In fact, those who escaped while on release or who were removed from the project because of infractions recidivated at the same rate as those who completed the work-release program. Thus, if work-release is preferred as an offender manpower service, it is apparently because of its relatively low (net) cost rather than its impact on employability.

In recent years attention has increasingly turned toward the use of post-release supportive services to facilitate the transition from institutionalization to society. Sometimes these services represent a continuation of pre-release manpower programs, but more commonly they are an alternative rather than a complementary undertaking. That these services are barely adequate is illustrated by the parole experience.

Each year about one-fourth of all prisoners in federal and state correctional institutions are conditionally released—that is, released on parole.[15] For these ex-offenders, the initial source of supportive service is the parole officer. Yet the extent to which parole officers actually aid the labor market experiences of prison parolees is miniscule. In the United States the ratio of parole officers to parolees is about one to sixty, barely half the optimal standard recommended by the President's Commission on Law Enforcement and the Administration of Justice.[16] Further, even though many parolees have obtained a prearranged job prior to parole—indeed, this is often a requirement for parole—the parole officer typically serves as a counselor or advisor, one who deals with psychological and/or behavioral problems, rather than one who seeks to facilitate employment. Such size and functional limitations on the manpower services provided by parole officers may be especially unfortunate, given the cruciality of the immediate post-release period for ex-offenders.

For other persons released from prisons and for some parolees, initial supportive services may be provided by family and friends or by a local community organization—for example, a half-way house. By the end of the 1960s, about 100 community institutions were available for prison parolees, and an unknown number for nonparoled releases.[17] However, such institutions typically serve other clientele in addition to ex-offenders, usually operate on only a very limited scale, and provide relatively few services, most of which are unrelated to employment. These characteristics, together with the opposition to community institutions that occasionally arises among local area residents, further indicate the difficulties encountered in attempting to improve the labor market experiences of ex-offenders.

One program of post-release supportive services that has received evaluative attention is Project Develop, conducted between 1966 and 1968 by the New York State Division of Parole.[18] This project furnished a group of 17-to-23-year-old parolees with counseling, education, vocational guidance, training, work orientation, placement, support, and follow-up assistance. Program completers were referred to trade schools, antipoverty organizations, and union- or MDTA-sponsored training. Compared with a control group having similar characteristics, project completers experienced substantially lower (though not statistically significant) rates of parole violation and recidivism. Unfortunately, detailed unemployment data were unavailable as the program essentially focused on the reduction of recidivism. In addition, however, the control group was matched to the completer group rather than to those originally enrolled in Project Develop. Had the latter served as the basis of comparison, the controls "would have done better on the average than those receiving services."[19]

Some manpower programs for offenders have explored the use of income supplements during the early stages of the post-release period. In the Rikers Island project, for example, small loans ranging from $50 to $200 were made to program participants, though their impact on subsequent labor market experience was not discerned. In the Draper Project, relocation allowances averaging $90 were given to trainees, but those monies were generally dissipated on nonessential items. One study of 250 offenders who completed various vocational rehabilitation programs and subsequently received cash payments of about $1,000 apiece concluded that these supplements "did no good. . . . Sometimes clients could not make the transition from the structured environment of prison to the competitive free world, from the excitement of crime to the less sanguinary pleasures of a 'square-jober' life, no matter how much money was available to them."[20] A more recent study that investigated the combined effects of employment assistance and income supplements found no significant differences between a control group that received none of these services and experimental groups receiving one or the other or both services respectively.[21] So far, then, the notion that income supplements (or outright cash payments) will have a positive effect on post-release labor market experiences of ex-offenders is not substantiated by empirical evidence.

The objective of any manpower training or supportive service program is, of course, to enhance the recipients' employability. Yet with reference to ex-offenders, the attention paid to job development and placement can best be described as meager.[22] Only about half of all federal prison releasees have prearranged jobs. Of these, less than 20 percent were secured with the assistance of public agencies. At a generous estimate, perhaps one in ten former prisoners receives Employment Service aid in locating their first job, and hardly any turn to the ES for assistance in subsequent job search. Of those offenders who do find jobs, less than one-quarter utilize experience or training acquired during institutionalization. While one can hardly pretend that a majority or even a large proportion of the institutionalized, many of whom are unskilled and uneducated, would be significantly aided by improved job development and placement services, there is reason to believe that, under proper conditions and in conjunction with other activities, such services can be more beneficial than suggested by the data presented above.

Consider, for example, experiences resulting from placement services provided as part of the MDTA prison projects.[23] Overall, the U.S. Employment and Training Service, which was charged with providing a wide range of pre-through-post-release services, was able to assist only a third of the trainees by itself, and an additional 7 percent by combining its efforts with those of the MDTA staff. Nineteen percent of the trainees obtained only an ES referral; 10 percent received no placement services; the remainder were helped by other agencies. Expectations that new jobs for ex-offenders would be created by the ES through elimination of barriers to employment were not borne out. However, when more intensive manpower serivces were provided—that is, when jobs were developed—the employment experiences of ex-offenders improved. Specifically, those persons placed in developed jobs had significantly more full-time employment, less unemployment, and more training-related employment than persons who obtained other (nondeveloped) jobs. Moreover, the data suggest that, with respect to the placement of ex-offenders, the Employment Service is more effective when it takes an active role rather than relying on standard procedures.

Despite the apparent success of intensive placement and job development services for prisoners trained under MDTA projects, these services are not widely provided. While several rationales have been offered for this lack of service expansion (for example, the experimental nature of the program, the

34

geographical isolation of most prisons, uncertainty of release, and so on), a main factor seems to be the "unwillingness of the ES staff to take on new functions."[24] The shortcomings of the ES, which stem in large part from structural and functional limitations, are well known, and need not be reviewed here.[25] When all is said, local ES offices are generally reluctant to offer ex-offenders anything but the standard assistance, services that do not facilitate job placement or the acquisition of training-related positions.

It is unclear whether the very limited effectiveness of job development and placement services for ex-offenders stems from the comparative irrelevance of the services or, instead, is due to the inadequacy of existing delivery systems. For example, in a pretrial intervention program conducted in New York City by the Vera Institute of Justice, young first-time offenders were provided a variety of employment-related services, mainly intensive group counseling, job development, and placement. In the case of program participants, court judgments were suspended for three months; for some program completers, charges were dropped.[26] Although this project clearly focused on a disadvantaged clientele, it was quite selective in determining whom to serve. To be eligible, offenders were required to be New York City residents; male; between 16 and 45 years old; unemployed or, if employed, earning no more than $125 weekly; not addicted to drugs; not charged with homicide, rape, or assault; and not previously imprisoned for more than one year. Understandably, these requirements eliminated about 90 percent of the offender group. Nevertheless, of those selected for the project during the first two years, 50 percent were black and a third were Puerto Rican; the average age was 21 and the average schooling was tenth grade; all had labor market problems; and, despite extensive efforts to screen out drug users, about a fourth were dependent upon drugs. Of the project's first 850 participants, 463 were referred to employment or training on at least one occasion, and of these, 309 were placed. But about half of those referred were sent to at least two employers, and one-third of the placements needed to be placed a minimum of two times.

In general, and despite the intensive job development services provided in this project, the labor market experiences of offenders were disappointing. An evaluative study of the Manhattan project found that at least half of the program participants were unemployed or their labor force status unknown.[27] Many of the offenders were dissatisfied with the jobs they obtained, and employers were not overly sanguine about the kinds of workers (or, more accurately, work) they received.

Some cost-benefit data for this project were also generated, but the underlying procedures were weak and the results inconclusive.[28] The project seemed to affect recidivism favorably, with participants experiencing a significantly lower rate than a comparably matched control group. However, the project's selection procedures confounded attempts to ferret out the independent effects of the manpower services provided. Further, drug users dropped out of the program at a relatively high rate and were more likely than nonusers to be rearrested. As in other instances, however, the Manhattan project expanded and, in fact, has spurred similar efforts in New York City.

Another pretrial intervention program, Project Crossroads, provided better information regarding measurement of performance.[29] This project's clientele were also disadvantaged, consisting largely of young nonwhite males with less than a high school education, low earnings, and substantial unemployment. Those who participated in the project benefited significantly, as indicated by their wage levels, employment status, and occupational distribution one year after completion. Recidivism was also reduced, but only in the short run. After one year, the recidivism rate for "experimentals" was about 20 percentage points higher than the rate for "controls."

While the impact of Project Develop on some measures of employment and recidivism was statistically significant, the magnitudes were not large. A sophisticated cost-benefit analysis of this project yielded a range of ratios comparable to those obtained for Job Corps, though some of the assumptions underlying the analysis were quite tenuous.[30] On balance, programs like Project Develop, "while they are worthwhile, have only a modest impact; . . . not too much should be expected from offender manpower programs which serve this group."[31]

What, then, may be concluded from our review of manpower services for the institutionalized? First, where discernible, the impact of these services on subsequent labor market experiences and recidivism is, at best, only marginal; relative to those who do not receive these services (that is, control groups), no significant impact obtains. More important, perhaps, our ability to judge the results of manpower programs for institutional populations is constrained by the lack of requisite program evaluations and by the presence of overly simple evaluations. Second, expectations about the potential impact of manpower programs on the labor market experiences of the institutionalized should be tempered by the realization that the data reviewed here pertain to programs operationalized during a period of economic expansion and tight labor markets—indeed, the tightest labor markets since the Korean War.[32] Is it likely that more positive outcomes will result during economically less ebullient times? Additionally, too heavy an emphasis on traditional manpower services for offenders, the mentally ill, the disadvantaged, or other labor force groups blurs the recognition that fundamental economic and political forces weigh heavily on the fortunes of the labor force, especially its peripheral components. It has repeatedly been observed that disadvantaged persons and, more generally, marginal labor force adherents make their greatest gains during periods of sustained economic growth.[33] These considerations suggest that ex-offenders and others on the periphery of the labor force may be aided by forms of "supported work," with the type and extent of support varying according to economic conditions.*

Finally, current manpower programs for the institutionalized tend to have a static one-dimensional focus. They ignore the dynamics of institutionalization and, not incidentally, the labor market. Thus, in what follows, we outline a flow model of the institutionalization process, and then suggest some of its implications for employment and the role of labor market information.

---

*A major development and research effort in the area of supported work is being launched with federal government and Ford Foundation support.

36

MODELING THE INSTITUTIONALIZATION PROCESS

A flow model of institutionalization must rest on recognition of the interlinkages between component parts of the institutionalization process. Thus, in attempting to determine the employment effects of manpower services for offenders, one cannot rely solely on data pertaining to program inputs and subsequent labor market experiences. Instead, consideration must be given to the important individual, organizational, and environmental factors that impinge upon the institutional dynamic.

Characteristics of the Institutionalized

Consider first the nature of the "material" with which total institutions are confronted. In general, and especially in the case of offenders, institutionalized people are notably disadvantaged. Relative to the general population, they tend to be disproportionately young, male, nonewhite, undereducated, and drug-addicted.[34] This profile by no means describes all institutionalized populations; there are, of course, a variety of types that may differ in any or all of these characteristics. Further, the sorting process makes some attributes more characteristic than others with regard to institutionalized populations. For example, young first-offenders tend to be placed in juvenile detention facilities, to receive shorter sentences, and to be on probation or parole proportionately more than older offenders.[35] Nevertheless, it is the case that the institutionalized remain a relatively disadvantaged group.

This conclusion is more strongly reinforced when we consider the labor market experiences and the alternatives to institutionalization for those who have been subsequently institutionalized. Offenders are, by and large, unsuccessful in the world of work. A survey of federal prison releasees with a median age of 29 showed that more than 10 percent had never been employed and more than half had been employed for less than two years cumulatively prior to incarceration.[36] Part of this low level of labor force activity stemmed from earlier criminal involvements. Additionally, offenders who worked prior to commitment were disproportionately represented in unskilled and semiskilled jobs and had only about two-thirds the earnings of all private nonagricultural workers.

The path leading toward institutionalization is irregular and the process selective. Although data on this point are sketchy, it appears that, at most, one-half of all offenses are reported; one-fifth are cleared by arrest; less than three-fourths of the adults and one-half of the juveniles arrested are convicted; and one-third of those convicted are sentenced to correctional institutions.[37] For every 100 crimes, then, two people are sent to prison. In the criminal justice system, institutionalization thus becomes subject to many factors, including seriousness of the crime, the nature of the evidence, perceived chances for rehabilitation, access to legal assistance, influence and social standing, and, of course, luck. There seems little doubt that whatever the

injustices or capriciousness of the system, those who are most disadvantaged are "selected" for incarceration.

Our comments suggest that the characteristics, experiences, and attitudes
of persons who eventually become institutionalized are such that they would
have severe employment problems even if they were not institutionalized, and
that manpower services aimed at improving their labor market potential have
but limited chances for success. The problem is worse when the disadvantaged
are also, even if only briefly, institutionalized.

Institutionalization and Its Impact

In total institutions, such as prisons, all phases of life are carried on in the
same place and under the same authority; members are treated similarly, if not
identically, their activities are carried out collectively; all aspects of daily
activity are tightly controlled and derive from explicit formal rulings mandated
by a group of officials; and enforced activities are subsumed under a single,
overriding plan that reflects the aims of the institution.[38] Perhaps the major
distinguishing characteristic of total institutions, however, is the socialization
process, sometimes described as "mortification":

> The stripping process through which *mortification of the self* occurs
> are fairly standard in our total institutions. Personal identity equip-
> ment is removed, as well as other possessions with which the inmate
> may have identified himself. . . . Standardized defacement will
> occur. . . . Family, occupational and educational career lines are
> chopped off, and a stigmatized status is submitted. Sources of
> fantasy materials which had meant momentary releases from stress in
> the home world are denied. Areas of autonomous decision are
> eliminated. . . . Many channels of communication with the outside
> are restricted or closed off . . . and the effect of each of these
> conditions is multiplied by having to witness the mortification of
> one's fellow inmates.[39]

Now total institutions do differ in their degree of totality. For example,
prisons are generally regarded as more total than mental hospitals, and the
latter more so than religious orders or the military.* In particular, institutional
totality tends to be a function of recruitment—that is, voluntary, semivoluntary
or involuntary recruitment—and of permeability—that is, the extent to which
social standards in the outside society influence those maintained within the
institution. In general, though, total institutions have a peculiar and significant
impact upon their inmates—an impact quite distinct (and probably opposite)

---

*It is interesting to speculate about the extent to which differences in institutional
totality differentially affect the labor market experiences of persons who leave these
institutions. Comparison of the job search and employment experiences of former prisoners,
priests, servicemen and mental patients might be especially illuminating in this regard.

from that resulting from manpower programs or rehabilitative activities generally. The design and evaluation of manpower services for offenders, mental patients, or other institutionalized populations thus appears seriously incomplete without consideration of the peculiar effects of institutionalization per se.

Post-Release Experiences

Following release, a large portion of the formerly institutionalized must cope with the labor market. How successfully they accomplish this is a crucial consideration in terms of evaluating the impact of pre-release manpower services or other factors. Success in the labor market may be determined in part by identifying the jobs, the wage rates, the earnings, and the unemployment experienced by formerly institutionalized persons following release. These data should be obtained at specified post-release intervals—say, three, six, and twelve months—and related back to manpower inputs, individual and institutional characteristics, and other variables. Naturally, comparably matched control groups are an integral part of the evaluative process.

Stating the ideal, however, does not mean that it is followed in practice. Like other U.S. manpower programs, those aimed at institutional populations generally do not provide for built-in evaluation or research, or for the guidance of policy through research. Evaluation—scientific, longitudinal evaluation rather than descriptions of how programs are operationalized—usually occurs in only a few instances, sometimes long after the fact, and generally on the basis of separate funding or individual research grants.[40] Is it little wonder, then, that one federal legislator recently remarked:

> One of the things that appall me about our government programs is we just don't know how well they're doing. You can go out in the field and you can get anecdotal examples of how we're succeeding ... but you can't get any data to back them up. ... This is what's missing in so many programs. ... We know how much we're spending on manpower; we don't know how many persons are being trained and finding jobs, improving their position, and so on.[41]

Knowledge of the post-release labor market experiences of the institutionalized can be refined even beyond the limits suggested above. Identification of job type, for example, facilitates analysis of the relationship between training and work specialty. Identification of jobs previously held (following release) allows for analysis of mobility patterns. More basically, identification of job search processes of the formerly institutionalized provides the data necessary to understand how these people deal with real-world labor markets. Evidence on this last point is fragmentary, but it suggests that informal sources and channels of labor market information are especially important for the formerly institutionalized.[42]

A major determinant of the employment experiences of the previously institutionalized (and, indeed, of all labor force groups) is the nature and functioning of the labor markets to which they are exposed. All but a few institutional releases are likely to be concerned with local as opposed to regional or national labor markets. The former differ considerably in their industrial and employment composition. Some markets are heavily service-oriented; others are dominated by heavy manufacturing industries; still others are characterized by a large proportion of government employment.[43] How do these structural differences affect the employment prospects of ex-offenders or mental patients? Some U.S. cities have high wages and high unemployment, while others have low wages and low unemployment.[44] Do the formerly institutionalized do better in the former kinds of market or (as one might predict) in the latter?

Search costs may also vary between different labor markets. In some, such as the San Francisco Bay area, the Employment Service seems to provide relatively good placement services.[45] In other areas, however, less favorable results obtain. How would these differences affect the willingness of institutional releases to use the Employment Service? Some cities provide guidance and counseling specifically for the formerly institutionalized; others do not. Again, one may question how search processes and employment "success" are differentially affected by these labor market characteristics.

Hiring and Selection Practices

Quite apart from their personal characteristics, the impact of institutionalization, or the manpower and/or supportive services provided them, the labor market experiences of the formerly institutionalized may be significantly affected by employer hiring and selection practices. For example, though they rarely have a blanket (or written) policy against the employment of ex-offenders, both private and public employers specify job "qualifications" that have the same effect as formal employment bars. A survey of private employers revealed that lack of education, failure to participate in rehabilitation programs, and a record of recidivism were the most frequently cited reasons for not employing ex-offenders.[46] Also important were the applicant's attitude toward work and authority and a record of robbery and drug-related violations.

There are licensing and bonding requirements in relatively few areas of commercial activity, but where they exist they virtually preclude the hiring of ex-offenders. Bonding is required for some service and retail jobs, and bonding companies are less than eager to cover those with criminal records. Where licenses are required (and there are about 7 million people employed in such occupations), possession of a criminal record is likely to render it difficult, if not impossible, for a person to obtain a license. Proof of "good moral character" frequently accompanies these requirements, and a criminal record is considered *prima facie* evidence of bad or at least unsuitable character. Furthermore, driver's-license "requirements" mandated by employers for various jobs work a hardship on—that is, deny employment opportunities to—former prisoners who, as a result of typical governmental statutory and administrative policies are either temporarily or permanently unable to claim (or reclaim) their driving privileges.

Public employers, who might be thought to be more amenable than others to employment of the formerly institutionalized, are, in fact, anything but that.[47] Virtually all governments at any level ask a job applicant about his or her offense record. Over half of the states and counties, and more than three-quarters of the cities, require disclosure of arrest records whether or not followed by conviction. While few public jurisdictions automatically exclude ex-offenders, many deny employment to those regarded as inferior by dint of their "infamous conduct." In many of these governments, an incorrect answer to a question on an application form provides the justification for rejecting an applicant. The dilemma faced by former prisoners concerning the truthfulness of responses versus the necessity of employment is well documented,[48] and makes particularly insidious the exclusionary practices based on an arrest record or the failure to report such record. Finally, about 90 percent of the major government employers solicit photographs from prospective applicants, and about half ask for fingerprints. This information is routinely referred to the FBI or the local police, and may well result in the exclusion from employment of those with arrest or conviction records.

The point of these comments is that whatever the importance of other factors, employer hiring and selection practices may significantly affect the labor market experiences of the formerly institutionalized. This is especially true when labor markets are loose, for then "qualifications" rise and people at the rear of the labor market queue (including those not previously institutionalized) suffer most. Hiring requirements are strangely contravened by cyclical changes in the economy, and these are importantly linked to the labor market experiences of formerly institutionalized persons.

SUMMARY

We have conceptualized the process of institutionalization as a dynamic flow model consisting of a series of key interlinkages (Figure 2.1). Major elements in the flow process are (a) the socioeconomic and attitudinal characteristics of the institutionalized, especially their pre-institutional labor market experiences, (b) the institutional experience, including exposure to manpower programs and services where available, but primarily to the various unique characteristics of "total" institutions, (c) the post-release labor market experiences of the formerly institutionalized, (d) the structure and functioning of local labor markets, particularly urban markets, and the mechanisms by which labor market information is transmitted to the formerly institutionalized individual, and (e) employer personnel practices, especially hiring and selection practices, and, relatedly, the degree of labor market tightness.

41

FIGURE 2.1

Flow Model of the Institutionalization Process

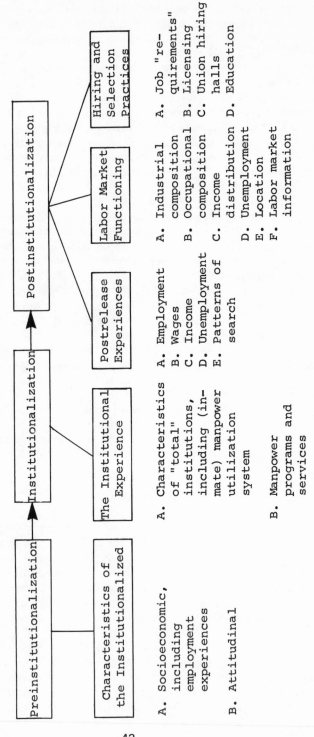

Our review of U.S. manpower programs for the institutionalized suggests that, rather than deriving from the dynamic model elucidated above, these programs generally have a static orientation. They appear to rest on the assumption that the provision of a lumpy investment (for example, in vocational training, remedial education, or supportive services) to the offender or mental patient augments the individual's quality and thus his salability in the labor market. The various factors—linkages—that might affect the labor market experiences of the formerly institutionalized, however, make this assumption dubious, if not harmful. Thus, it is not surprising, perhaps, that, on the basis of available evidence, manpower programs for the institutionalized have at best only a marginal positive impact on those receiving these investments and, more generally, no significant impact relative to nonrecipients.

Apart from their immediate interest, these findings take on greater significance when related to larger issues of social policy and social research—for example, the considerable controversy that has raged for several years concerning the role of busing in achieving equal educational opportunity. Many arguments and many policies were established on the assumption that racial segregation in large part "explained" black-white differences in educational achievement specifically and social and economic conditions generally.[49] Presumably, integration was required to overcome these inequalities, and in the schools, one (but by no means the only) way of effectuating integration was through housing. Yet, the effect of busing-induced integration on academic achievement (and, for that matter, on aspirations, self-concept, and race relations) is uncertain. One investigator concludes:

> If the justification for mandatory busing is based upon an integration policy model . . . , then the justification has to be called into question. The data do not support the model on most counts. . . . [M]andatory busing for purposes of improving student achievement and interracial harmony is not effective and should not be adopted at this time.[50]

Needless to say, these conclusions are also the subject of much controversy.[51] But, they indicate that major social ills are, if not incurable, certainly intractable, and that manipulation of any single variable in a dynamic, multidimensional process is likely to have, at best, only limited impact. Clearly, this observation is consistent with the Coleman Report[52] and, more recently, with the work of Jencks and his colleagues, who demonstrate that income equality by no means results from equalizing educational attainments.[53] Indeed, there is as much or more occupational and income variation within education levels as between them. The continuing controversy over the relative importance of heredity and environment generally further indicates the stubborn nature of what we choose to call social problems,[54] just as recent analysis of the shift from a centralized to decentralized—that is, "community-controlled"—school districts in New York City underscores the limits of unidimensional public policies conceived without proper regard for the dynamic nature of social processes.[55]

43

The limitations of single-factor approaches to major social problems have recently been explicated by Peter Marris, a Britisher. Commenting on social experimentation in the United States during the 1960s as well as the negative and the inconclusive findings resulting from evaluations of federal programs, Marris remarks:

> ... These disappointments were, I think, inevitable. ... [P] rojects undertaken seldom derived from any plan, but were negotiated piecemeal in response to individual initiative, the available funds, political pressure, or the prejudices of sponsors. . . .[56]

These policy "failures" have a more basic genesis, however. Specifically, in approaching social reform,

> ... we risk being misled by an analogy with applied science, which confuses the issues and produced unhelpful conclusions. . . . [S]ocial improvement cannot be routinized after the manner of a research and development laboratory. . . . [S]ocial policy cannot avoid questions of power and interest. . . . [A]nd it seems inherently improbable that any particular constellation of factors . . . which determine aggregate social behavior . . . will remain stable for long.[57]

Marris concludes by noting that to justify an experiment, one must take a stand on questions of value and belief, an exercise that essentially commits one to the value of experimentation itself. This may be a fundamentally useful objective, however, because it develops understanding of the process of change and tests government's (and ultimately society's) adaptability to change.[58]

Returning to the immediate subject of analysis, it may be suggested that manpower programs designed to provide services for the institutionalized, while generally formed without sufficient recognition of the dynamics of institutionalization, nevertheless have promoted greater understanding of the processes of change in total institutions and of the interactions between these institutions and the rest of U.S. society. As regards the adaptiveness of government and society to these changes, we should note that, in the treatment of the insane, the criminal, the orphaned, the delinquent, and the poor, we are continuing to move away from, rather than toward, institutionalization. Finally, within the parameters of institutionalization, there is heightened appreciation of the limits of single approaches or even alternative philosophies of treatment. Thus, in commenting on the field of corrections, one authority notes that the current trend is to

> ... think small and stay out of people's lives as much as we can. We must aim not to do good but to minimize harm. There is nothing glorious about this proposition. . . . But perhaps the idea of doing the least possible damage is just what we, our courts, and our legislators, must learn.[59]

In a field so often characterized by optimistic overstatement and exaggerated claims of success, such an observation is not to be taken lightly.

The dynamic model of institutionalization developed here may be used to explore further the labor market experiences of the formerly institutionalized, as will be attempted in the next chapter. Consistent with the theme of this book, we focus particularly on the role of labor market information (and the channels through which it is transmitted) in aiding the institutionalized who seek employment in the urban economy.

NOTES

1. See U.S. Bureau of the Census, *The Statistical Abstract of the U.S.* (Washington, D.C.: Government Printing Office, 1973), pp. 77, 160-61; U.S. Department of Justice, Law Enforcement Assistance Administration, *1970 National Jail Census* (Washington, D.C.: LEAA, February 1971), pp. 2, 9; U.S. Department of Health, Education and Welfare, *Statistics on Public Institutions for Delinquent Children*, 1970 (Washington, D.C.: National Center for Social Statistics, June 30, 1971), pp. 3, 10; David J. Rothman, "Prisons, Asylums, and Other Decaying Institutions," *The Public Interest,* 26 (Winter 1972): 4.

2. See U.S. Bureau of the Census, loc. cit.

3. George A. Pownall, *Employment Problems of Released Prisoners* (Washington, D.C.: U.S. Department of Labor, Manpower Administration, 1969), p. 12.

4. Clyde E. Sullivan and Wallace Mandell, *Restoration of Youth Through Training* (New York: Wakoff Research Center, 1967).

5. Robert Taggart III, *The Prison of Unemployment: Manpower Programs for Offenders* (Baltimore: The Johns Hopkins Press, 1972), p. 43.

6. Abt Associates, Inc., *An Evaluation of the Training Provided in Correctional Institutions Under the Manpower Development and Training Act, Section 251*, Final Report, Vols. I, II, and III (Washington, D.C.: U.S. Department of Labor, Manpower Administration, Office of Policy, Evaluation and Research, March, April, and May 1971).

7. Abt Associates, op. cit., Vol. III, p. 15. For a more detailed analysis of this study's shortcomings, see David Lewin, "Memorandum for Record Concerning the Evaluation of MDTA-Funded Experimental Training Programs in Correctional Institutions Performed by Abt Associates" (New York: Columbia University, October 1971). (Mimeo.)

8. Garth L. Mangum, "Manpower Research and Manpower Policy," in *A Review of Industrial Relations Research, Volume II*, Benjamin Aaron et al., eds. (Madison, Wis.: IRRA, 1971), pp. 87, 100.

9. Observe the changes in characteristics of trainees enrolled in MDTA training programs between 1963 and 1972, as reported in U.S. President, *Manpower Report of the President—March, 1973* (Washington, D.C.: Government Printing Office, 1973), statistical appendix, pp. 231-34.

10. John M. McKee *The Draper Project: MDTA Experimental and Demonstration Findings, No. 6* (Washington, D.C.: U.S. Department of Labor, Manpower Administration, 1971).

11. Pownall, op. cit., p. 98.

12. Taggart, op. cit., p. 61.

13. Abt Associates, Inc., op. cit., Vol. II, pp. 36-37.

14. J. Kitchener and W. Lebowitz, "Preliminary Highlights from Work-Release Follow-Up Study" (Bureau of Prisons, March 1970). (Mimeo.)

15. See U.S. Bureau of the Census, op. cit., p. 160. Of the 233,121 "departures" from federal and state prisons in 1970, 58,911 were conditional.

16. President's Commission on Law Enforcement and the Administration of Justice, *The Challenge of Crime in a Free Society* (Washington, D.C.: Government Printing Office, 1967), pp. 167-70. The Commission recommended that "all jurisdictions should examine their need for probation and parole officers on the basis of any average ratio of 35 offenders per officer . . ." (p. 167).

17. International Half-Way House Association, *1969 Directory* (Cincinnati, Ohio: The Association, 1969).

18. Leonard Witt, *Project Develop* (New York: New York State Division of Parole, 1969).

19. Taggart, op. cit., p. 67.

20. E. M. Oliver et al., *A Future for Correction Rehabilitation?* (Olympia, Wash.: Division of Vocational Rehabilitation, Coordinating Service for Occupational Education, 1969), p. 60.

21. K. J. Lenihan, *Study of Effects on Ex-Prisoners of Financial Aid and Employment Assistance Programs Designed to Facilitate Post-Release Adjustment*, preliminary findings reported to the author by the Manpower Administration, U.S. Department of Labor, Spring 1973.

22. Data in this section are based on Pownall, op. cit., pp. 130-79.

23. Data in this section are from Abt Associates, op. cit., Vol. II, pp. 78-86.

24. Taggart, op. cit., p. 76.

25. Compare with Stanley H. Ruttenberg and Jocelyn Gutchess, *The Federal-State Employment Service: A Critique* (Baltimore: The Johns Hopkins Press, 1970), passim.

26. Vera Institute of Justice, *The Manhattan Court Employment Project* (New York: Vera Institute of Justice, 1970). Unless otherwise noted, this source provides the data for subsequent discussion in this section.

27. Ibid., and Vera Institute of Justice, "Final Report of the Manhattan Court Employment Project" (December, 1971), pp. 25-26. (Mimeo.)

28. Vera Institute of Justice, "Quarterly Report, March 1, 1971 to June 30, 1971," passim. (Mimeo.)

29. Analysis in this section is based on Roberta Rovner-Pieczenik, *Project Crossroads as Pre-Trial Intervention: A Program Evaluation* (Washington, D.C.: National Committee for Children and Youth, 1970).

30. See John F. Holahan, *A Benefit-Cost Analysis of Project Crossroads* (Washington, D.C.: National Committee for Children and Youth, December

1970); and Glen G. Cain, *Benefit-Cost Estimates for Job Corp*, discussion paper (Madison, Wis.: Institute for Research on Poverty, 1967).

31. Taggart, op. cit., p. 34.

32. See *Manpower Report of the President*, p. 127; U.S. Council of Economic Advisers, *Economic Indicators, April, 1973* (Washington, D.C.: Government Printing Office, 1973), p. 11. Between 1966 and 1969 aggregate U.S. unemployment rates of 3.8, 3.8, 3.6 and 3.5 percent respectively were recorded. These compare with rates of 4.9 percent in 1970, 5.9 percent in 1971, 5.6 percent in 1972, and 5.0 percent as of this writing (spring 1973).

33. See, for example, Dale L. Hiestand, *Economic Growth and Employment Opportunities for Minorities* (New York: Columbia University Press, 1964).

34. Pownall, op. cit.; Daniel Glaser, *The Effectiveness of a Prison and Parole System* (Indianapolis, Ind.: Bobbs-Merrill, 1964), pp. 316-40.

35. Taggart, op. cit., pp. 8-10.

36. Pownall, op. cit., pp. 166-80.

37. Taggart, op. cit., p. 6.

38. See the classic statement by Erving Goffman, "The Characteristics of Total Institutions," in *A Sociological Reader on Complex Organizations*, 2d ed., Amitai Etzioni, ed. (New York: Holt Rinehart and Winston, 1969), p. 314.

39. Ibid., pp. 317-18.

40. Mangum, op. cit., passim. On the analytics of evaluation, see Michael E. Borus and Charles G. Buntz, "Problems and Issues in the Evaluation of Manpower Programs," *Industrial and Labor Relations Review*, 25 (January 1972): 234-45.

41. Elizabeth Drew, "A Reporter at Large: Conversations with a Senator," *The New Yorker*, May 19, 1973, pp. 119-20.

42. Glaser, op. cit., pp. 214-19; Pownall, op. cit., pp. 137-39.

43. Thomas M. Stanback, Jr., and Richard V. Knight, *The Metropolitan Economy: The Process of Employment Expansion* (New York: Columbia University Press, 1970), pp. 116-56.

44. On this point, see Stanley L. Friedlander, *Unemployment in the Urban Core: An Analysis of Thirty Cities with Policy Recommendations* (New York: Praeger, 1972); also Robert E. Hall, "Why Is the Unemployment Rate So High at Full Employment?" *Brookings Papers on Economic Activity, 3, 1970* (Washington, D.C.: The Brookings Institution, 1971), pp. 369-402, esp. 375-84.

45. Margaret Thal-Larsen et al., *Placement and Counseling in a Changing Labor Market: Public and Private Employment Agencies and the Schools*, Report of the San Francisco Bay Area Placement and Counseling Survey (Berkeley: Institute of Industrial Relations, University of California, August 1970).

46. John McKee et al., *Barriers to the Employment of Released Male Offenders* (Elmore, Ala.: Rehabilitation Research Foundation, 1970), p. 22.

47. The discussion in this section relies primarily on Institute of Criminal Law and Procedure, Georgetown University Law Center, *The Effect of a*

Criminal Record on Employment with State and Local Public Agencies (U.S. Department of Labor, Manpower Administration, May 1971).

48. See Glaser, op. cit., pp. 233-38.

49. This "model" is explicated in David J. Armor, "The Evidence on Busing," *The Public Interest*, 28 (Summer 1972): 92-97.

50. Ibid., pp. 114-16.

51. See, for example, Thomas F. Pettigrew et al., "Busing: A Review of 'The Evidence,'" *The Public Interest*, 30 (Winter 1973): 88-118; David J. Armor, "The Double Standard: A Reply," *The Public Interest* 30 (Winter 1973): 119-31.

52. James S. Coleman et al., *Equality of Educational Opportunity* (Washington, D.C.: Government Printing Office, 1966).

53. Christopher Jencks et al., *Inequality: A Reassessment of the Effect of Family and Schooling in America* (New York: Basic Books, 1972).

54. Compare with Arthur Jensen, "How Much Can We Boost I.Q. and Scholastic Achievement?" *Harvard Educational Review* 39, no. 1 (Winter 1969): 1-123; and Richard J. Herrnstein, "On Challenging an Orthodoxy," *Commentary*, 55 (April 1973): 52-62.

55. Diana Ravitch, "Community Control Revisited," *Commentary*, 53 (February 1972): 69-74.

56. Peter Marris, "Experimenting in Social Reform," n.d., p. 4. (Mimeo.)

57. Ibid., pp. 2, 5, 6, 7.

58. Ibid., pp. 12-15.

59. David J. Rothman, "The Correction of Practices of Correction," review in the *New York Times Book Review*, May 27, 1973, p. 14.

3

INFORMATIONAL FLOWS
AND LABOR MARKET
INTERMEDIARIES FOR
THE INSTITUTIONALIZED

In recent years, various analysts have pointed to the importance of information in facilitating the smooth functioning of labor markets.[1] If job vacancies exist and qualified applicants are seeking work, it is presumably the absence (or high cost) of information that prevents the matching of labor supplies with demands. Refining this simple model, Yavitz and Morse identify a narrower concept, the "job market," and note that critical intermediaries in the informational system act to "significantly modify the flows and arrivals of the two main inputs into the job market."[2]

With respect to the formerly institutionalized, it appears that their labor market experiences and, more generally, their ability to return to society, are fundamentally affected by "critical intermediaries." In the case of ex-offenders, for example, several intermediaries—family and friends, probation and parole officers, guidance counselors and community institutions (for example, half-way houses)—serve as labor market surrogates, essentially bearing the costs of job search, information acquisition, and job development.

To illustrate the dynamics of this process and the role of labor market information, we will focus in this chapter on the behavior of ex-offenders and labor market intermediaries in the country's largest and most complex urban economy, New York City. Urban labor markets are especially a subject of concern, because they are the types of market that the institutionalized are most likely to encounter after release. The chapter is organized as follows: First, we describe some characteristics of New York City correctional institutions and their inmate populations. Then we explicate the job search behavior of formerly institutionalized persons in New York City and analyze the provision of labor market information through key intermediaries. Finally, we indicate how the labor market behavior of the formerly institutionalized and the functions required of labor market intermediaries are critically affected by the inmate manpower utilization system of correctional institutions. This analysis flows logically from the dynamic model of institutionalization presented in Chapter 2.

CORRECTIONAL INSTITITIONS AND THE INSTITUTIONALIZED IN NEW YORK CITY

The stocks and (particularly) flows of institutionalized populations are not always easily discerned. Available data indicate that more than 12,000 persons were imprisoned in New York City at the end of 1970 (Table 3.1).[3] Of this total, approximately 95 percent were incarcerated in institutions operated by the city's Department of Corrections; the remainder were housed in county jails.[4]

Inmates of New York City correctional institutions are virtually evenly divided between those serving sentences and those awaiting disposition of their cases. Although women constitute less than 5 percent of the city's inmate population, only about 40 percent of them are serving sentences, compared with more than 50 percent of the men. Among the nonadolescent detention institutions, the largest population is in the Brooklyn house, followed closely by the Manhattan house (The Tombs). The N.Y.C. Correctional Institution for Men has the largest population among all city institutions, and about 200 city inmates are in hospital prison wards.

In general, persons serving sentences in city correctional institutions have been convicted of misdemeanors or other relatively minor crimes. Individuals convicted of felonious offenses are sent to New York State maximum- or medium-security correctional institutions (Table 3.2), virtually all of which are located in upstate New York. In 1971 some 12,500 persons were incarcerated in state correctional institutions.

From a labor market perspective, of course, the flows of the institutionalized are more important than the stocks. In New York City, more than 1 million criminal offenses were reported in 1970, and more than 378,000 arrests were made in connection with these offenses.[5] About two-thirds of the arrests were for misdemeanors and related crimes; the remainder, for felony violations. While some charges are dropped, some arrestees released on bail, and other arrestees not necessarily confined, these data suggest a substantially greater inmate load (even if many confinements are of the short-term variety) in New York City detention and correction facilities than is discernible from institutional stock data.

Further, our analysis indicates that several hundred thousand persons annually become inmates, even if only briefly, of correctional institutions in New York City. Only a relatively small proportion of this group remains institutionalized for more than a year. The remainder quickly flow out of these institutions, returning to the larger society and, presumably, the labor market. It should be noted, however, that the flow of both short-term and long-term residents of correctional institutions to New York City may be even greater than previously suggested.

TABLE 3.1

Inmates in N.Y.C. Department of Correction Institutions and County Jails Located in New York City, by Status and Institution, December 31, 1970

Institution	Total Present		Awaiting Court Disposition		Serving Sentences	
	Male	Female	Male	Female	Male	Female
Total, all institutions	11,292	798	5,754	585	5,538	213
Total, county jails	296	260	296	260	–	–
Total, detention institutions	5,597	–	5,070	–	527	–
N.Y.C. Adolescent Remand Shelter	1,672	–	1,606	–	66	–
Branch Queens House of Detention for Men	24	–	–	–	24	–
Bronx House of Detention for Men	887	–	791	–	96	–
Brooklyn House of Detention for Men	1,262	–	1,178	–	84	–
Manhattan House of Detention for Men	1,225	–	1,054	–	171	–
Queens House of Detention for Men	527	–	441	–	86	–
Total sentence institutions	5,205	496	210	285	4,995	211
Brooklyn Community Residential Facility	22	–	–	–	22	–
N.Y.C. Correctional Institution for Men	4,098	–	48	–	4,050[a]	–
N.Y.C. Reformatory for Men	1,085	–	162	–	923	–
House of Detention for Women	–	496	–	285	–	211[b]
Total hospital prison wards	194	42	178	40	16	2
Bellevue Hospital	90	5	74	3	16	2
City Hospital at Elmhurst	–	37	–	37	–	–
Kings County Hospital	104	–	104	–	–	–

Note: Dash (–) represents zero.

[a] Includes 2,780 sentenced inmates lodged at state prison correctional facilities.

[b] Includes 49 sentenced female inmates lodged at Westfield State Farm.

Source: Derived from New York State Division of the Budget, *New York State Statistical Yearbook, 1972* (Albany: Publications Office, August 1972), pp. 252, 254.

TABLE 3.2

Inmates under Custody in N.Y.S. Correctional Institutions, by Reason for Commitment and Sex, December 31, 1970

Reason for Commitment	Total		Male		Female	
	Number	Percent	Number	Percent	Number	Percent
Total commitments	12,579	100.0	12,210	100.0	369	100.0
Felonies	10,771	85.6	10,526	86.2	245	66.4
Murder	742	5.9	727	6.0	15	4.1
Manslaughter and abortion	1,593	12.7	1,505	12.3	88	23.9
Rape	248	2.0	248	2.0	–	–
Felonious assault	688	5.5	671	5.5	17	4.6
Robbery	3,528	28.0	3,497	28.6	31	8.4
Burglary[a]	1,179	9.4	1,178	9.7	1	0.3
Burglar's tools[b]	7	*	7	0.1	–	–
Grand larceny (not auto)	589	4.7	565	4.6	24	6.5
Grand larceny (auto)	125	1.0	123	1.0	2	0.5
Negligent homicide	42	0.3	40	0.3	2	0.5
Kidnaping	36	0.3	35	0.3	1	0.3
Dangerous weapons	288	2.3	286	2.4	2	0.5
Dangerous drugs	1,085	8.6	1,036	8.5	49	13.3
Forgery	184	1.5	176	1.4	8	2.2
Sex offenses, except rape	194	1.5	194	1.6	–	–
Criminal possessing stolen property	77	0.6	77	0.6	–	–
Arson	86	0.7	84	0.7	2	0.5
Fraud	1	*	1	*	–	–
All other felonies	79	0.6	76	0.6	3	0.8

Misdemeanors and violations in 552 CCP

	Number	Percent	Number	Percent	Number	Percent
Unlawful entry[a]	9	0.1	9	0.1	—	—
Burglar's tools[b]	6	*	6	*	—	—
Jostling	1	*	1	*	—	—
Criminal possessing stolen property	10	0.1	10	0.1	—	—
Sex offenses	9	0.1	8	0.1	1	0.3
Dangerous drugs	40	0.3	36	0.3	4	1.1
Dangerous weapons	11	0.1	11	0.1	—	—
Escaped prisoners	6	*	3	*	3	0.8
Other misdemeanors and violations	284	2.3	264	2.2	20	5.4
Petit larceny	136	1.1	123	1.0	13	3.6
Unauthorized use of motor vehicles[c]	46	0.4	45	0.4	1	0.3
Assault, 3rd degree	39	0.3	37	0.3	2	0.5
Prostitution and vice	2	*	—	—	2	0.5
All other misdemeanors	61	0.5	59	0.5	2	0.5
Other						
Youthful offenders	812	6.4	783	6.4	29	7.9
Wayward minors	33	0.3	14	0.1	19	5.1
Juvenile delinquents	12	0.1	12	0.1	—	—
Not convicted[d]	503	4.0	462	3.8	41	11.1
Data not available	72	0.6	65	0.5	7	1.9

(first data row of group: 92, 0.7 | 84, 0.7 | 8, 2.2)

Note: Dash (−) represents zero. Asterisk (*) indicates less than 0.1 percent.

[a] Unlawful entry, committed on or after September 1, 1967, included in burglary.

[b] Possession of burglar's tools, committed on or after September 1, 1967, no longer a felony.

[c] Unauthorized use of motor vehicle, committed on or after September 1, 1967, no longer grand larceny (auto).

[d] Certain insane or mental defectives and transfers from departments of Mental Hygiene and Social Services.

Source: New York State Division of the Budget, *New York State Statistical Yearbook, 1972* (Albany: Publications Office, August 1972), p. 249.

Persons incarcerated in the New York Metropolitan area and, indeed, outside of the area, may nevertheless seek employment in New York City subsequent to release. This would most likely occur in cases where the institutionalized were originally residents of the city. As we note later in this chapter, the formerly institutionalized rely heavily on family and friends in seeking employment, particularly during the immediate post-release period. Thus, if a person from New York City is confined in a maximum-security correctional institution located in upstate New York, he is nevertheless likely to return to the city and seek employment through a network of personal relationships. So, too, this may occur among persons incarcerated in New Jersey, Connecticut, and Eastern Pennsylvania, suggesting a substantial flow of formerly institutionalized persons to New York City.[6]

A second factor contributing to an enlarged estimate of the formerly institutionalized in the New York City labor market is the secular deemphasis of institutionalization as a method of treating offenders.[7] This trend, observable throughout the United States, is, as evidenced by the data in Table 3.3, occurring in New York. Concomitant with the relative decline of institutionalization is, of course, the growing emphasis on community-based treatment for offenders.

In sum, hundreds of thousand persons are exposed annually to varying degrees of incarceration in New York's correctional institutions. Most of these individuals are institutionalized for relatively short periods and return quickly to society and the labor market. Additionally, long-term residents of total institutions are increasingly returning to their communities, as localized treatment gradually replaces institutionalization. Finally, the flow of ex-offenders and other formerly institutionalized people to New York City may be augmented even further by the opportunities for "losing one's past" that are afforded in a large, complex urban society.

LABOR MARKET IMPERATIVES AND
THE FORMERLY INSTITUTIONALIZED

In Chapter 1 we reviewed some of the major characteristics of the New York City labor market. Our analysis suggests that institutional releasees (and others) who enter the New York City labor market confront an urban economy characterized by substantial proportions of financial, producer, and government services, as well as wholesale and retail trade, and relatively little manufacturing. More important, the occupational structure that emerges from this industrial composition is one in which white-collar, professional, and credentialed positions occupy a prominent role. About 16 percent of New York City's jobs are in the professional, technical, and kindred category, 8 percent are managerial and proprietary types, 27 percent are clerical, 7 percent sales, and 14 percent service positions (see Table 1.5).

Many, indeed probably most, of these occupations are simply not realistic employment alternatives for the institutionalized, even for those who might aspire to them. Substantial educational attainment is a prerequisite for employment in scientific occupations, such as chemistry and engineering; in the "independent" professions of law, medicine, and dentistry; in accounting and architecture; and in the major governmental functions of education and social welfare. The institutionalized rarely possess these credentials and, more rarely still, the resources required to achieve them.

Additionally, occupational licensing presents formidable barriers to the employment of the formerly institutionalized. Nationally, approximately 7 million people work in licensed occupations.[8] In New York City as elsewhere, "physicians, dentists, lawyers, accountants, architects, and engineers all require some form of state license to practice. Public school teachers ... require licensing ... and the same may be said for other professionals working for government in New York City."[9] Licensing requirements are by no means limited to professional occupations; they may also impinge upon employment in a service capacity or in wholesale and retail trade. Thus, in New York:

> ... a major impediment to employment faced by ex-offenders is the Alcoholic Beverage Control Law which provides that a business licensed by the State Liquor Authority (SLA) may not employ in any capacity a person convicted of a felony or of certain enumerated offenses. Since businesses licensed by the SLA include hotels, restaurants, supermarkets and many department stores, the current statute prohibits employment of ex-offenders in many of the low-skilled jobs to which most ex-offenders must resort for lawful employment.[10]

The bars to employment for other formerly institutionalized persons (for example, mental patients), while generally less overt than for ex-offenders, are everpresent and, because of their subtlety, might be more difficult to deal with. Further, the formerly institutionalized can be denied access to positions as craftsmen, foremen, and operatives in industries, such as construction and apparel manufacturing, where union membership is a prerequisite to employment.[11] Craft union membership is not easily gained, even by the noninstitutionalized, during prosperous times, let alone in periods of loose labor markets.

Finally, institutional releasees can be specifically barred from some types of government employment in New York City. Conviction of a crime classified as a felony or petty larceny, for example, renders one ineligible for employment with the city's police department.[12] Commission of misdemeanors or repeated offenses may bar persons from employment as firemen and as policemen as well, for these violations make it less likely that one will survive the "background investigation" routinely conducted as a requirement for entry into the city's protective services. And, of course, the formerly institutionalized face that omnipresent bugaboo: falsifying (or not truthfully answering) employment application forms in seeking employment in the urban economy. New York City's instruction to applicants for the position of sanitationman that "any willful mis-statement will be cause for disqualification" is by no means the only such requirement in this urban labor market.[13]

The foregoing discussion indicates that the formerly institutionalized who seek employment in New York City are effectively barred from many

55

TABLE 3.3

Number of Inmates under Custody in Correctional Institutions,
by Institution and Sex, December 31, 1964-71

Institution	1964	1965	1966	1967	1968	1969	1970	1971
All institutions	19,439	19,073	16,417	14,670	13,381	12,998	12,579	12,525
Males	18,510	18,219	15,729	14,129	12,945	12,604	12,210	12,148
Females	929	854	688	541	436	394	369	377
Maximum security correctional facilities	10,906	10,845	10,080	9,132	8,379	8,401	8,528	8,251
Attica	2,042	2,083	2,041	1,831	1,658	2,039	2,230	1,104
Auburn	1,637	1,651	1,602	1,543	1,558	1,667	1,553	1,575
Clinton	2,114	2,123	1,886	1,497	1,362	1,124	867	962
Green Haven	2,076	1,995	1,749	1,653	1,725	1,725	1,919	1,906
Great Meadow	1,213	1,169	1,020	1,043	721	635	908	1,247
Ossining	1,824	1,824	1,782	1,565	1,355	1,211	1,051	1,457
Medium security correctional facilities	4,918	4,846	4,421	3,916	3,523	3,184	2,811	2,959
Clinton D & T Center[a]	–	–	50	94	97	89	94	78
Coxsackie	709	746	606	550	533	474	500	525
Eastern[b]	589	619	599	822	727	553	–	–
Elmira	1,448	1,380	1,214	1,196	1,054	1,085	1,012	1,070
Glenham[c]	–	–	–	–	–	–	228	263
Reception Center at Elmira	378	316	325	309	266	247	234	220
Wallkill	505	497	492	483	470	405	434	488
Woodbourne[d]	626	675	546	–	–	–	–	–
Bedford Hills (female)[e]	500	460	455	343	296	269	219	315
Western (female)[f]	163	153	134	119	80	62	90	–

Minimum security correctional facilities	321	301	324	321	334	351	329	322
Camp Pharsalia	73	59	79	74	71	75	81	74
Camp Monterey	64	69	65	69	68	78	64	67
Camp Summit	94	84	86	96	98	99	102	87
Camp Georgetown	90	89	94	82	97	99	82	94
Institutions for the retarded	54	73	141	165	305	460	456	450
Beacon	54	71	139	163	290	438	420	421
Albion (female)f	—	2	2	2	15	22	36	29
Institutions for the mentally ill	940	866	948	993	983	1,105	2,597	2,843
Dannemora	343	346	402	394	400	449	1,028	1,062
Matteawan	597	520	546	599	583	656	1,569	1,781
Males	535	462	485	541	519	579	1,364	1,544
Females	62	58	61	58	64	77	205	237

Note: Dash (—) represents zero.

aClinton Diagnostic and Treatment Center created June 21, 1966.

bEffective September 23, 1970, Eastern Correctional Facility used to house New York City inmates only. Called Catskill prior to July 8, 1970.

cBeacon (borderline) prior to July 8, 1970.

dEffective October 31, 1967, Woodbourne temporarily turned over to Narcotic Addiction Control Commission.

eWestfield Prison and Reformatory prior to July 8, 1970.

fEliminated as of June 7, 1971 as a result of legislative action on the Governor's budget.

Source: New York State Division of the Budget, *New York State Statistical Yearbook, 1972* (Albany: Publications Office, August 1972), p. 248.

jobs—jobs generally characterized by "high wages, good working conditions, employment stability, chances of advancement, and equity and due process in the administration of work rules."[14] In other words, once released, the institutionalized are, in large part, denied access to primary labor markets. For this reason, and also, of course, because of their many other disadvantages and the dysfunctional behaviors encouraged by total institutions, the formerly institutionalized must seek employment principally in secondary labor markets or in those narrow channels of the primary market where entry restrictions are minimal and *about which information is available*. These observations lead quite naturally to an analysis of the job search behavior of the formerly institutionalized and, concomitantly, of the role of labor market intermediaries.

MARGINS OF SEARCH AND LABOR MARKET SURROGATES

The ex-offender or former mental patient who seeks employment in New York City is likely to be concerned with "intensive" rather than "extensive" margins of search, and to prefer informal over formal sources of labor market information. These two dimensions of search are, of course, interrelated.[15]

With respect to margins of search, it is not especially useful to the institutional releasee to know (or attempt to find out) about a variety of job vacancies in the city or the range of wage rates typically offered by different employers for the same job. As noted earlier, because of "qualifications" and other barriers to employment, some vacancies do not represent true job openings for the formerly institutionalized. Additionally, in a complex urban area such as New York City, some job vacancies, which the formerly institutionalized might feel qualified to fill, might be so far removed from place of residence that transportation costs would become prohibitively high.

Sometimes a model of the labor market is posited in which an individual seeking employment in a particular specialty searches far and wide for the best offer (that is, "quotation"), for which the wage rate serves as a proxy, and then selects the best alternative. Apart from the fact that the formerly institutionalized are not likely to search for work in markets that are national or regional in scope, they are also likely to disavow extensive search in the local market. Modifying Rees' discussion of this point, the problem facing the formerly institutionalized individual "is not to get in touch with the largest possible number of potential [employers]; rather, it is to find a few [employers] promising enough to be worth the investment of thorough investigation."[16] Thus, the formerly institutionalized can be expected to pursue intensive job search within narrow but nevertheless relevant markets.

Informal sources of labor market information are, in general, most germane to intensive search activity; this is especially so for the institutionalized. In contrast, because they provide broad, extensive information and do not furnish specialized services, formal informational sources are used hardly at all by the formerly institutionalized. For example, ex-offenders, are reluctant to use the Employment Service and, furthermore, do not hold it in high

58

regard.[17] That this perception is not entirely misplaced is reflected in a recent evaluation of the local job bank program in ES offices:

> The researchers concluded that present job banks are not achieving more efficient man-job matching, nor are they improving service to the disadvantaged, reducing frictional unemployment, or maintaining or increasing ES volume on overall activity measures (placements, openings, etc.). The authors also perceived a willingness on the part of Manpower Administration officials to "accept facts and implications associated with positive findings and not to accept those associated with negative findings."[18] [quotations in original]

The New York State Employment Service (NYSES) reports that only about 1,000 ex-offenders used its New York City facilities in 1971.[19] The ES placed about one-third of those persons, but because follow-up data were not obtained, it is impossible to determine how long the formerly institutionalized were employed and what degree of "success" they subsequently experienced. Among those not placed, roughly 27 percent were referred but not hired, and for another 24 percent no suitable job openings were found. Finally, approximately 400 ex-offenders referred to the NYSES by probation and parole authorities did not report to the service.

That the formerly institutionalized rely heavily on informal sources of labor market information is not surprising when related to the job search behavior of blue-collar and low-wage workers generally. A variety of studies have demonstrated that these workers place primary reliance on informal information sources when seeking employment.[20] Formal sources of labor market information—employment agencies, newspaper advertisements, college placement offices, and so on—tend to be used by white-collar and professional workers predominantly. The formerly institutionalized are perhaps unique, however, in the extent to which they make use of informal sources of information and particularly in their reliance on labor market intermediaries.

THE INTERMEDIARIES

Family and Friends

There is little question that formerly institutionalized persons seeking employment in New York City use family and friends as a major source of labor market information. This conclusion emerges from discussions with staff members of the City's Department of Corrections and NYSES personnel.[21] Family and friends are cheap sources of information, and, more important, they provide the kind of data most relevant to the institutional releasee: the fairness of the employer, chances of long-term employment or mobility, kinds of co-workers, proximity to residence, willingness to hire ex-offenders, and so on. When obtaining a job with a friend's employer, the formerly institutionalized

59

person is able to maintain a personal friendship and have regular access to a source of moral support, not small considerations in reintegrating with work or society. In addition, family and friends are likely to know the capabilities and experiences of the institutionalized person.

Whether or not they would choose to rely so heavily on family and friends as sources of labor market information, the institutionalized are pushed in this direction by the procedural requirements and circumstances of institutionalization. Consider, for example, that in New York State (and City), one of the main factors governing parole decisions is the offender's ability to secure employment prior to release—that is, to pre-arrange a job.[22] Clearly, with few resources of his own and restricted freedom, the offender has an obvious incentive to pursue gainful employment through personal relationships. Family and friends who are called upon to aid the offender in this way not only provide labor market information but also perform the matching function. They are thus not merely information channels but also labor market surrogates.

As in New York, family and friends elsewhere serve as labor market intermediaries for the institutionalized.[23] A recent study of federal prison releasees found that over 80 percent of those with pre-arranged jobs located them through friends, family, and former employers. Of the jobs so obtained, more than 85 percent were operative, service, or unskilled types. Interestingly, of the relatively few white-collar and skilled blue-collar positions pre-arranged for federal prisoners, less than 60 percent were obtained through personal relationships.

Following release (and, most noticeably, after a job previously secured has been lost), ex-offenders continue to search for employment through networks of personal relationships. As described by Glaser:

> Friends, relatives and former employers are the major job sources. Whenever releasees need employment their procedure is to make contact with everyone whom they know is working and ask if his employer is looking for more men or if he knows of any place else that is hiring. Leads on possible job opportunities are also voluntarily conveyed to the unemployed releasees by friends and relatives. Apparently, when these informal procedures fail to yield employment, the releasees are most likely to make the rounds of large firms or other possible employers on a hunch basis. This direct confrontation of a prospective employer is involved in more job placements than are any of the formal mediators between employee and employer, such as private employment agencies or correctional officials.[24]

Probation and Parole Officers

While probation and parole officers serve as sources of labor market information much less often than family and friends, they are nevertheless important potential sources of information because they are the major link between the criminal justice system and the offender following conviction (in the case of probation) and incarceration (in the case of parole).

In New York City as in other parts of the United States, the role assigned to probation and parole personnel incorporates a peculiar blend of custodial and treatment behaviors. On the one hand, there is the need to obtain information about the post-sentencing or post-prison conduct of the offender so as to aid the courts and parole boards in determining whether probationary or parole status should be continued. On the other hand, probation and parole officers are supposed to facilitate and meliorate the transitions between a partially or completely restricted status and total freedom by providing assistance and rule enforcement.

In addition to the structual demands of the probation and parole officer's job and the manner in which these impinge upon post-institutional treatment of offenders, there are also different "styles" of probation and parole supervision to consider. Following one typology, we can identify (1) the punitive officer, who attempts to coerce the offender via threats and punishment, thus to protect the community, (2) the protective agent, who, because of his vacillating between protection of the community and protection of the offender, engages in ambivalent supervisory practices ranging from praise to punishment, and (3) the welfare worker, whose principal concern is his "client," and who perceives himself as providing emotionally neutral diagnostic treatment.[25] The combination of structural and attitudinal determinants of probation and parole officer behavior suggests the possibility of vastly different consequences for individual offenders. By and large, the custodial approach seems to predominate over treatment- or quasi-treatment-oriented approaches, but, even where the latter are followed, the relative amount of attention paid to employment and, more generally, the labor market, is small.

In New York City's Department of Probation, for example, interview data reveal a mixture of treatment and custodial practices.[26] There is constant checking on the activities of released offenders, including visits by probation personnel to home, school, or work, and recording of these activities in permanent files. At the same time, probation and parole officers are almost continuously counseling and advising offenders, providing a mixture of social support and warnings about behavioral proprieties. Frequently, members of the department act as mediators in disputes between offenders and friends, family, occasionally employers, and sometimes even other components of the criminal justice system.

More important, New York City's Probation Department also provides some labor market services. A few offenders are referred to assessment centers, such as the Bedford-Stuyvesant Restoration Corporation. Others are placed on jobs in companies with which the Department has managed to establish a "feeder" relationship—for example, Ideal Toy Co. Some probation and parole officers actively search the labor market for job opportunities congruent with the skills of the offenders they supervise. In other instances, offenders are referred to community institutions, training centers, and government-operated manpower programs. Finally, the Probation Department maintains formal ties with the NYSES, the Urban

League, and several private employment agencies, once again referring offenders to these organizations.

Thus, our analysis indicates that, in New York City, probation and parole officers sometimes serve as a source of labor market information. In this, they act as intermediaries between offenders and employers. Furthermore, a few officers are able to develop jobs and arrange employment for offenders. Here, the officer extends his role to that of labor market surrogate, searching along the intensive margin in the local labor market as a representative of the offender. In this capacity, furthermore, the officer approximates the role played by family and friends in the experiences of the institutionalized. However, in New York City (and in the United States, generally) the dual nature of the probation and parole officer's job, the diversity of attitudes among occupants of these positions, and the restrictions imposed by typically heavy case loads, combine to make the labor market an ancillary rather than a central concern of probation and parole personnel.[27] For the purposes of our analysis, then, these officers are best viewed as potential rather than actual surrogates for offenders in the labor market.

Community Institutions*

As mentioned earlier in this chapter, there is a discernible trend away from conventional institutionalization and toward community-centered approaches in dealing with problems of offenders and other traditionally institutionalized groups. The data in Table 3.3 illuminate the nature of the trend in New York State. In New York City there are far more than 100 community institutions, both public and private, currently operating in the corrections and mental health fields.

The identification of a community as the locus of treatment for criminal offenders or the mentally ill suggests implications for labor market behavior. Specifically, when treatment (or even custody) is localized, the ability of the institutionalized to pursue intensive margins of search is apparently enhanced. This localization can be accomplished in either of two ways: first, in a community-based nonincarcerative facility, the "institutionalized" person has available opportunities to undertake search on his own; second, where the community-institution acts as a surrogate for the offender or mental patient, search can be carried out in the local market and, more narrowly, within key avenues of the local market. Presumably, one reason for the lack of much effort devoted to labor market activities by the staffs of large state prisons and mental hospitals, or the lack of success when effort is devoted, is the remoteness of the institutions from the relevant—that is, local—markets.

---

*In this section, our focus expands beyond correctional institutions and ex-offenders to include the mentally ill and the institutions relevant to this group. This occurs partly because of the nature of our empirical work, but more basically because of the generalizability of the analysis in this and subsequent sections.

To what extent do community-based correctional and mental health institutions in New York City facilitate, either directly or indirectly, the search for employment? The most accurate response to this question is that we do not know. There seems to be no central registry or data source indicating the number of persons treated by New York City's community-based institutions, let alone the labor market-related activities of these institutions.[28] Nevertheless, we will present some overall impressions concerning community-based organizations and then review an active labor market program in one of these institutions.

In general, and especially in recent times, the concept of community-based treatment has seemed particularly appealing.[29] Further, as a philosophy of treatment, it rivals its predecessors, the "custodial" and "rehabilitative" schools, in major historical significance. Yet, community-based treatment is not a new idea, having been "advocated in the reform literature for at least 50 years."[30] Many communities have opposed localized treatment facilities, despite apparent cost savings, and legislatures are reluctant to appropriate funds for them. Most germane, perhaps, the available evidence indicates that—in the area of corrections, for example—community-based treatment is no more successful than conventional approaches, at least as measured by recidivism.[31]

These comments should not be taken to mean that community-based treatment for offenders or the mentally ill is an unwise strategy or that it cannot succeed. Rather, we are suggesting that this approach is not the panacea implied by some of its advocates. In New York City, for example, some community institutions service several different types of clients. While this might seem humane, and it enhances an institution's diversity, it also creates important problems of treatment, administration, and evaluation. Community-based institutions offer a social system that contrasts sharply with that of conventional incarcerative institutions; yet not all offenders, mental patients, drug addicts, or otherwise disadvantaged people respond similarly (that is, favorably) to such an environment. Finally, in pursuing multiple objectives— that is, in attempting to provide social, psychological, economic, and other types of support to offenders and the mentally ill, community-based institutions are likely to tax their own resources severely, to be all-encompassing in a society that encourages pluralistic affiliations, and, more important from the present perspective, to make subordinate the attainment of gainful employment in a hierarchy of objectives.

Having pointed to some seldom articulated problems of community-based institutions, let us now consider one institution that does make the labor market a major focal point of its treatment efforts: namely, Fountain House.[32] This community organization, founded in New York City in 1948, was formed to provide a place where discharged psychiatric patients could adjust to community life. The program is entirely voluntary, and between 70 and 100 patients per month are referred to Fountain House by New York State hospitals, the State Division of Vocational Rehabilitation, and other agencies. Fountain House's employment-related activities are twofold: First, it actively involves members in the daily management and operation of its facilities. Some patients prepare food, others perform housekeeping duties, still others attend to clerical functions, and tasks are rotated. Then, after a period of participation in that phase, members may move into the transitional employment program. The staff of Fountain House has identified or developed more than 50 positions in local industry and has secured commitments from employers to hire Fountain House members. The jobs are regular positions carrying standard rates of compensation, but the Fountain House staff has access to them in order to provide on-the-job assistance as required to members. Employees referred by Fountain House are free to leave their jobs after a three-to-four-month period. Employers participating in the program have expressed strong approval of the project and of the performance of personnel obtained through it. A recent HEW-sponsored evaluation of this program yielded several positive outcomes, although some of the findings are inconclusive and others are negative.[33]

The Fountain House experience suggests that, in some circumstances, community-based organization, such as half-way houses, day-care centers, and localized treatment centers, can provide employment assistance to the formerly institutionalized and perhaps even serve as labor market surrogates for these individuals. A strong emphasis on the labor market would involve community organizations in job search, information acquisition, job development, and post-employment assistance. In general, however, and on the basis of our review of the New York City experience, community-based correctional and mental care centers have such a broad range of goals and, less frequently, such a diverse clientele that a concern for employment is often subordinate to other objectives. Consequently, as with probation and parole officers, community-based treatment organizations are at present potential more than actual labor market intermediaries for the formerly institutionalized.

We have examined the labor market behavior of formerly institutionalized persons in New York City, pointing out the special importance of intensive job search and informal sources of labor market information for these individuals. Further, we have identified several key labor market intermediaries for offenders and, in one instance, for the mentally ill and elucidated the surrogacy role undertaken by family and friends, and, less frequently, by probation and parole officers and community institutions. In relation to the flow model of institutionalization outlined in Chapter 2, this analysis is clearly concerned with "labor market functioning." Yet, our analysis would be incomplete, and, moreover, our understanding of the problems faced by labor market intermediaries who attempt to aid the formerly institutionalized would be thwarted, were we not to consider one of the earlier variables in the dynamic flow model: namely, "the institutional experience."

INMATE MANPOWER UTILIZATION
IN CORRECTIONAL INSTITUTIONS

The importance of the systems of manpower utilization[34] in a prison (or other total institution) stems not from any of its characteristics per se but, rather, from the way in which these characteristics diverge from those of manpower utilization systems in more conventional worlds of work. In Chapter 2 we outlined the peculiar nature of the socialization process in total

institutions and the implications of this process for programs of inmate rehabilitation. The following analysis suggests a more general "unresolved conflict
between the requirements of custody and treatment." Specifically:

> ... it would seem logical that life within a correctional institution
> should, as nearly as possible, be like that of any normally decent
> community outside ... not only ... on humanitarian grounds but
> also because a normal community life in prison provides a milieu that
> is as likely to be antithetical to criminal behavior as would be the
> removal of ghetto conditions outside. . . .[35]

Further:

> The impossibility of accomplishing this in any suitable degree is what
> has led many to feel that prisons as they now exist should be
> abolished.[36]

Viewed from this perspective, manpower utilization systems in total
institutions are similarly antithetical to those on the outside—or, more accurately, to some of those on the outside. Specifically, the former promote
behavior patterns consistent with secondary (and perhaps even tertiary) rather
than primary labor markets, thus making it less rather than more likely that a
released offender or mental patient will be able to cope successfully with life
on the outside.[37]

In the following sections we present some of the characteristics of these
manpower utilization systems.

Compensation

A considerable amount of work goes on in prisons, much of it performed
by the institutionalized. A large portion of this work involves maintenance of
the institution, of course, but some of it results in the production for sale of
goods and services. In 1970 about one-fourth of all federal prisoners were
employed by Federal Prison Industries, Incorporated.[38] In state institutions,
and in prisons generally, some type of work activity commonly occurs. Items
produced include machine parts, textiles, clothing, stamped metal goods, and
license plates, while services include furniture repair, laundering, and tire
recapping.

For maintenance-type work performed by the institutionalized, virtually
no compensation is paid, though there may be other rewards (and punish-
ments) associated with these activities. For "productive" work, wages typically
are paid, but these vary substantially and are frequently set by state law. One
study found that prisons pay their inmates between 10¢ and $1.00 per day for
work performed.[39] It is estimated that the average prison laborer earns
between 10¢ and 65¢ per day.[40]

Clearly, these wage rates are so low that they offer no real incentives and
may even serve as disincentives to work for those persons subsequently

released. More important, these wage levels do not even approach those that characterize low-wage employments in conventional labor markets. In 1971, for example, approximately 8 percent of full-time, year-round, privately employed workers earned less than $3,000 annually ($11.54 per day), and 14 percent earned less than $4,000 per year ($15.38 per day)."[41] In fact, among 25-to-64-year-old males heading poor families, about half work on a full-time, year-round basis. If these workers are considered poor and their employments characteristic of secondary markets, then institutional inmates may be regarded as impoverished and, on the basis of compensation received, concentrated in tertiary markets. Recognition of the dichotomy between wages paid to the institutionalized and wages paid even to those at the bottom of the U.S. occupational structure and of the implications of this dichotomy for programs of rehabilitation has recently led to a proposal that federal and state legislation be introduced "requiring that an inmate employed at productive work in a federal, state, or local institution . . . be paid no less than the minimum wage operative nationally or in his state."[42]

Compensation, of course, includes not only wages but also fringe benefits. In the private sector of the U.S. economy, fringes account for about 27.5 percent of total payroll costs, and in government roughly 28.2 percent.[43] While some total institutions—for example, the military—may provide relatively generous fringe benefits, incarcerative types do not. One does not expect paid vacations for prisoners or mental patients, but presumably sick leave, disability insurance, and some forms of seniority benefits could be envisioned as components of institutional compensation systems. Yet these are nowhere to be found in practice. Again, the importance of this observation stems not so much from recognition of institutional compensation practices per se but, rather, from the way these differ from compensation practices on the outside. In primary labor markets and, more important, in many secondary markets, fringe benefits are an important aspect of reward systems. This is not so for the institutionalized, however, even those engaged in the production of goods and services.

Work Scheduling

Working shifts and hours of work in total institutions are typically irregular and attenuated. This is understandable; it is primarily due to the imbalance between the supply of and demand for the outputs of these institutions. The excess supply of institutionalized labor is reflected in the large amount of idleness that still characterizes inmate populations. A study of MDTA-supported training in correctional institutions found only 14 percent of the "trainees" working in rehabilitation-oriented programs. Production-oriented programs were limited to very specific items produced in limited quantities for contract or in-house utilization.[44]

Among the inmates involved in these programs, 80 percent worked about half of what is regarded as a normal work week on the outside. Four percent

66

worked fewer than twenty hours per week, and 16 percent worked forty or more hours weekly. More important, in most projects:

> ... inmates rarely had a choice regarding particular work assignments. Work was either unavailable to all inmates (e.g. when manpower needs varied according to trends in seasonal demands) or was an institutional requirement which often resulted in "make-work" programs.[45]

Note, too, that because of poor management and antiquated equipment, "two or three inmates are assigned to do a task that would require only one worker in private industry."[46] Consequently, the hours of work of institutional inmates overstate the amount of work actually performed. As in the case of compensation, methods of work scheduling and the forced emphasis on artificial or "busy work" creates labor market behaviors that contrast sharply with those on the outside, including even some low-wage, casual (that is, secondary) jobs.

Mobility

One of the main characteristics of real world labor markets is their dynamism. Demands for and supplies of labor are constantly changing and, even where they appear static, there may be considerable underlying fluctuations. In the manufacturing sector of the private economy, for example, employment has remained relatively stable for the last several years, totaling roughly 19 million.[47] However, the manufacturing labor force has been in a considerable state of flux; between 1966 and 1972 turnover never averaged below 50 percent per year and occasionally approached 60 percent.[48] Not all of this turnover occurred because of worker preferences, of course. About two of every five separations were due to layoffs, deaths, or retirements. Nevertheless, approximately three-fifths of manufacturing turnover is voluntary in nature (as measured by quit rates).[49] More important, many workers who quit their jobs, whether in manufacturing or other industries, do so to take advantage of superior employment opportunities. This mobility—horizontal mobility—is an important aspect of labor market behavior.

In contrast, the inmate of a prison or the patient in a mental-care facility rarely has a chance for horizontal mobility. The institutionalized person's status is most likely to fluctuate between idleness and menial employment. Where employed, the individual is not free to leave one job and move to another within the institution or, indeed, to leave the job in preference for idleness. The latter is especially noteworthy when contrasted with the behavior of younger workers on the outside who have increasingly displayed a predilection for part-time employment and, concomitantly, voluntary labor force inactivity.

If opportunities for horizontal mobility for members of total institutions are virtually nonexistent, so, too, are chances for upward mobility. To what higher ranking position can an inmate of a correctional institution, assigned to a laundering detail, aspire? What chances for promotion are there for the mentally-ill individual performing custodial functions in his institution? Is there anything so mundane as job classification systems (and accompanying compensation plans) in total institutions? The negative answers to these questions put prisons, mental hospitals and the like, again, in marked contrast with the outside world, where opportunities for promotion and upward mobility generally characterize the employment scene. In fact, some have noted that the bulk of labor market activity in the economy is internal in nature.[50] There are relatively few "ports of entry" to employment, and, once the matching function has been performed in external markets, it is the internal market that becomes behaviorally meaningful. At least in the core economy, and to some extent in the periphery,[51] individuals move up in grade or to new positions, receive wage increases at reasonably regular intervals and, in general, are upwardly mobile. More important, perhaps, they aspire to upward mobility, though it is unclear to what extent this is a function of the chances for mobility. In total institutions, opportunities for mobility are unavailable, thus dampening any aspirations to mobility that might exist among the institutionalized.

Due Process

One of the significant aspects of employment relationships in the United States (and of those in industrialized countries, generally) is the extent to which authority is, if not bilateral, at least not totally unilateral. Workers have at their disposal a variety of appeals procedures that give them some measure of due process in their relations with employers. Where the work force is unionized, appeals systems take the form of formal grievance processes. These provide for representation, adjudication, application of discipline on the basis of contractual language and in relation to the offense, and, more generally, the joint settlement of industrial disputes. Furthermore, more than 95 percent of the grievance procedures in labor contracts in the United States provide for binding arbitration as the terminal step.[52] Workers and managements are thus ensured of a reasonably fair and impartial process with respect to settling problems of the workplace and have recourse to an independent judgment when the need arises.

Personnel systems also provide a measure of due process and protection against the vagaries of arbitrary authority. These systems emphasize, for example, hiring and selection on the basis of merit or achievement; they specify procedures and requirements that are, in general, applied uniformly to individuals or groups—though their impact may not be uniformly distributed among various groups. Job classification plans provide similar or identical job titles for persons performing the same duties, and individuals will be compensated on the basis of their classification, years of experience, and other clearly enunciated standards. In nonunion situations, personnel systems may also specify appeals procedures, complete with requirements for utilization, provisions for representations, and methods of adjudication.

In addition to grievance procedures and personnel systems, managerial authority is also constrained by custom and the informal bargaining so characteristic of employment relationships.[53] Overtime scheduling in industry, for example, is frequently done on the basis of seniority. Yet this practice had its genesis in the informal bargaining dynamic that historically occurred between foremen concerned with production scheduling and workers interested in the allocation of rewards. Practices in the areas of work assignments and job bidding, now regarded as established, similarly developed out of the configuration of employer and employee interests.

With respect to the nature of authority and appeals systems, the contrasts between total institutions and the outside world are manifestly obvious. In prisons and mental hospitals, in military institutions and religious orders, in any total institution, authority flows from the top down, is unilateral, and is not expected to be contravened. Moreover, the institution commands the power to enforce its will, and the use of this power to accomplish the intended purpose is sanctioned if not legitimated by society. In such an environment, appeals procedures, due process, and buffers against arbitrary or excessive authority are not likely to flourish.[54]

If the institution possesses generally unilateral authority, it is unlikely that modifications will occur in the sphere of work. If a prisoner in a state correctional institution is employed in metalworking for four hours per day, he is still under the supervision (and exposed to the same authority) of those who control his nonworking hours. The prison staff, and especially those who occupy the equivalent of first-line supervisory positions in industry—that is, prison guards—are not about to shift from custodial to rehabilitative treatment and back, according to the division between work and nonwork activity![55]

Indeed, it is much more likely that the authority relationships flowing from a custodial approach to institutional management will swamp those that stem from a treatment approach. Furthermore, as has been amply demonstrated, the level of resources devoted to truly rehabilitative activities in total institutions is simply not high enough to permit any but the most meager use of trained supervisory personnel for specialized activities. Consequently, the same individuals who exercise unilateral and frequently punitive authority over the institutionalized are also used to administer activities labeled "rehabilitative." It is not surprising, then, that appeals procedures, grievance systems, and other devices intended to meliorate absolute authority are uncharacteristic of total institutions, generally, or their (inmate) manpower utilization practices, specifically. Again, however, the important point is that these practices are atypical with respect to those that predominate in outside labor markets.

We have focused on systems of inmate manpower utilization in total institutions, arguing that their characteristics and the behaviors they promote are inconsistent with those typical of or required by labor markets, especially primary markets, on the outside. Thus, if one is to realistically discuss the employment experiences or potential employability of the institutionalized and the extent to which they may be aided by conventional labor market information, it must be recognized that the impact of institutionalization acts to worsen their chances for success subsequent to release. In a sense, institutionalization does provide labor market information, but it is of a negative type, for it cultivates and promotes behavior patterns that are dysfunctional in all but the most peripheral real world labor markets.

In particular, differences between institutional and "outside" manpower practices crystallize around concepts of *labor market dynamism* and *job rights*. In prisons (but also in mental hospitals, and perhaps in the military and religious orders as well), technology is typically stagnant and the capital-labor ratio exceedingly low, as is usually the case in undeveloped economies. In prisons, for example, "equipment on which the prisoner works is frequently antiquated and obsolete . . . and even where it is new, it is usually designed for a very restricted type of industrial production."[56] Manpower utilization in these institutions is not linked to dynamic product or labor markets. With excess labor supplies, not surprisingly, idleness, slovenliness, low wages, low (or nonexistent) mobility, and irregular work scheduling are the order of the day. As the National Council on Crime and Delinquency notes:

> . . . The whole prison operation lacks efficiency, incentives, production norms, and the complex of operational goals and attitudes that are the hallmark of a successful industrial endeavor. The knowledge of private business or organized labor is not involved in inmate training or industry operation.[57]

If business and labor are not solicited on matters of work practices, so, too, are they not approached on questions concerning employment relationships. In total institutions, authority is unilateral and pervasive. Conditions of incarceration, let alone employment, are not subject to formal negotiation nor reduced to writing. Appeals against arbitrary authority find none but the most explosive channels for their articulation. Incentive and reward structures might be altered suddenly and prior credits built up by individuals rendered useless. In sum, the totality of those conditions labeled job rights in conventional employment either do not exist or exist at only the most meager levels in total institutions.

The combination of the absence of job rights and the lack of access to dynamic or free labor markets in total institutions makes more evident that (a) the problems characteristic of these institutions are intractable; (b) limitations are inherently imposed upon rehabilitation programs operationalized in the institutional setting; (c) added difficulties are created for institutional releasees in coping with the labor market; and, most important, for purposes of our previous discussion; (d) burdens are imposed upon intermediaries who attempt to supply labor market information to the formerly institutionalized. It is no exaggeration—and may even refine an analytical concept—to suggest that total institutions develop tertiary labor markets and promote behaviors appropriate to such markets.[58] Unfortunately, and in contrast, it is primary and some secondary labor markets that exist on the outside and about which most information is generated.

SUMMARY

This chapter has explored the role and uses of labor market information by formerly institutionalized persons seeking employment in New York City. We began by describing characteristics of correctional institutions and the institutionalized in and around the New York area and then reviewed salient dimensions of the city's labor market. Next, we examined the job search behavior of ex-offenders in New York City, indicating that their search is conducted along intensive margins and is directed primarily towards informal sources of information. We noted the critical role of labor market intermediaries—family and friends, probation and parole officers, and community institutions—in the search patterns of the formerly institutionalized (not only ex-offenders), and suggested that occasionally but not typically these intermediaries serve as labor market surrogates for the institutionalized. A major factor limiting the extent to which intermediaries are able to assist the formerly institutionalized in the labor market is the nefarious impact of inmate manpower utilization systems in total institutions. These systems, characterized by stagnant economic conditions and a lack of job rights, promote behaviors that are dysfunctional for entry into primary and even some secondary labor markets.

The analysis presented here is based on a dynamic, multivariate flow model of the institutionalization process outlined in Chapter 2. This model, which points out crucial interlinkages between elements of the process, illuminates not only the difficulties involved in attempting to "solve" a complex social problem with single-dimension approaches but also the cumulative impact of intertwined individual, organizational, and environmental factors on the labor market and other experiences of the institutionalized. The dominance of these factors and their configurations is likely to render labor market information of limited value only for the formerly institutionalized who seek employment in the urban economy. This theme underlies our policy recommendations posited in Chapter 8.

NOTES

1. See George J. Stigler, "Information in the Labor Market," *Journal of Political Economy*, 70 (Supplement: October 1962): 90-105; Albert Rees, "Information Networks in Labor Markets," *American Economic Review: Papers and Proceedings of the Eighty-Fourth Annual Meeting* (May 1966): 559-66; Charles C. Holt, "How Can the Phillips Curve be Moved to Reduce Both Inflation and Unemployment?" in *Microeconomic Foundations of Employment and Inflation Theory*, E. S. Phelps, et al., ed. (New York: Norton, 1970), pp. 224-56.

2. Boris Yavitz and Dean W. Morse, *The Labor Market: An Information System* (New York: Praeger, 1973), p. 115.

3. Unless otherwise noted, all data in this section are from New York State Division of the Budget, *New York State Statistical Yearbook, 1972* (Albany: Publications Office, August 1972).

4. In early 1972, however, the inmate population of New York City Department of Correction facilities was reported as 14,000. Interview with Jack Dolan, Prison Health Services, April 6, 1972.

5. See New York State, Division of the Budget, op. cit., p. 246.

6. For example, New York State, Division of the Budget, op. cit., reports (in addition to the data already presented) more than 96,500 persons admitted to county jails in New York State and 8,000 admitees to county penitentiaries (pp. 252-53).

7. See David J. Rothman, "Of Prisons, Asylums, and Other Decaying Institutions," *The Public Interest*, 26 (Winter 1972): 3-17.

8. National Clearinghouse on Offender Employment Restrictions, *Offender Employment Review* (Washington, D.C.: NCOER, March 1972), p. 2.

9. See Marcia Freedman, "Opportunity and Income," in *New York is Very Much Alive*, Eli Ginzberg, ed., (New York: McGraw-Hill, 1973), p. 85.

10. National Clearinghouse on Offender Employment Restrictions, op. cit. p. 2.

11. Freedman, op. cit., pp. 81-82, 89-91.

12. See Bernard Cohen and Jan M. Chaiken, *Police Background Characteristics and Performance* (New York: The New York City Rand Institute, August 1972), Table 1, p. 4.

13. New York City Department of Personnel, Civil Service Commission Internal Memorandum concerning Notice of Examination for Sanitation Man, December 1969.

14. Peter B. Doeringer and Michael J. Piore, *Internal Labor Markets and Manpower Analysis* (Lexington, Mass.: Heath, 1971), p. 165.

15. See Albert Rees, "Information Networks in Labor Markets," *American Economic Review: Papers and Proceedings of the Seventy-Eighth Annual Meeting* (New York: American Economic Association, May 1966), pp. 559-66, for further elaboration of these concepts.

16. Ibid., pp. 561-62.

17. Interview with Ellison Ball, Director of Probation, New York City Department of Probation, June 30, 1972.

18. George P. Huber and Joseph C. Ullman, *A Study of the Local Job Bank Program: Performance, Structure and Direction*, reported in U.S. Department of Labor, Manpower Administration, "Summaries of R & D Reports, No. 9" (Washington, D.C.: Office of Research and Development, December 1972), p. 21.

19. Data in this section were obtained from an interview with Janet Piner, New York State Employment Service, New York City Office, July 24, 1972.

20. Rees, op. cit. pp. 559-66; F. T. Malm, "Recruiting Patterns and the Functioning of Labor Markets," in *Management of Human Resources*, F. T. Malm, Paul Pigors, and Charles A. Myers, eds. (New York: McGraw-Hill, 1964), pp. 242-56; Albert Rees and George P. Shultz, *Workers and Wages in an Urban Labor Market* (Chicago: University of Chicago Press, 1972), pp. 199-217.

21. Interviews mentioned above with Ellison Ball, New York City Department of Probation, Janet Piner, New York State Employment Service, and Jack Dolan, Prison Health Services, New York City Department of Corrections.

22. Interview with Ellison Ball, New York City Department of Probation, June 30, 1972. For a general treatment of this issue, see Daniel Glaser, *The Effectiveness of a Prison and Parole System* (Indianapolis: Bobbs-Merrill, 1969), Ch. 13. Note particularly Glaser's criticisms of pre-arranged employment for offenders (pp. 214-19).

23. The following data are from George A. Pownall, *Employment Problems of Released Prisoners* (Washington, D.C.: U.S. Department of Labor, Manpower Administration, 1969), pp. 136-38.

24. Glaser, op. cit., pp. 231-32.

25. Ibid., pp. 292-93.

26. Interviews with Ellison Ball, Director of Probation, New York City Department of Probation, June 1972.

27. For further analysis of the probation and parole function as well as data on case loads, see The President's Commission on Law Enforcement and the Administration of Justice, *The Challenge of Crime in a Free Society* (Washington, D.C.: Government Printing Office, 1967), pp. 162-70.

28. Interview with Bertram J. Black, Comprehensive Health Planning Agency, New York City, June 15, 1972.

29. See, for example, The President's Commission on Law Enforcement and the Administration of Justice, op. cit., pp. 165-66, 171-73; Board of Trustees, National Council on Crime and Delinquency, *Institutional Construction: A Policy Statement* (Paramus, N.J.: NCCD, April 1972).

30. David J. Rothman, "The Correction of Practices of Correction," review in the *New York Times Book Review*, May 27, 1973, p. 12.

31. Ibid., pp. 12-14; James Robinson and Gerald Smith, "The Effectiveness of Correctional Programs," *Crime and Delinquency* January 1971): 67-80.

32. For additional information on Fountain House and its transitional employment program, see Research Utilization Branch, Office of Research and Demonstration, Social and Rehabilitation Service, U.S. Department of Health, Education and Welfare, *Research and Demonstrations Brief*, no. 5 (October 15, 1971); Thomas Malamud, *An Evaluation of Rehabilitation Services and the Role of Industry in the Community Adjustment of Psychiatric Patients Following Hospitalization* (New York: Fountain House, 1969).

33. Malamud, op. cit.

34. This concept has its genesis in the more restricted notion of an industrial relations system first propounded by John R. Dunlop. See his *Industrial Relations Systems* (New York: Holt-Dryden, 1958), especially Ch. 1.

35. Albert Morris, "Correctional Reform: Illusion and Reality," in Massachusetts Correctional Association, *Correctional Research*, Bulletin No. 22 (Boston, Mass.: November 1972), p. 12.

36. Ibid.

37. These concepts are discussed in Michael J. Piore, "On the Job Training in the Dual Labor Market," in *Public-Private Manpower Policies*, A.

Weber et al., eds. (Madison, Wis.: IRRA, 1969), pp. 101-32; Peter B. Doeringer and Michael J. Piore, op. cit., pp. 164-83.

38. "Another Year of Success Reported in Training, Hiring of Prison Inmates," *Federal Times*, February 10, 1971.

39. Abt Associates, Inc., *An Evaluation of the Training Provided in Correctional Institutions Under the Manpower Development and Training Act, Section 251*, Report MEL 71-096 (Washington, D.C.: Manpower Administration, U.S. Department of Labor, April, 1971), p. 31.

40. Board of Trustees, National Council on Crime and Delinquency, *Compensation of Inmate Labor, A Policy Statement* (Paramus, N.J.: NCCD, April 25, 1972), p. 1.

41. Derived from U.S. Bureau of the Census, *Current Population Reports*, Series P-60, No. 85, "Money Income in 1971 of Families and Persons in the United States" (Washington, D.C.: Government Printing Office, 1972), Table 54, pp. 135-38.

42. Board of Trustees, National Council on Crime and Delinquency, op. cit., p. 2.

43. Edward H. Friend, *First National Survey of Employee Benefits for Full-Time Personnel of U.S. Municipalities* (Washington, D.C.: LMRS, October 1972), p. 3.

44. Abt Associates, op. cit., p. 30.

45. Ibid.

46. Board of Trustees, National Council on Crime and Delinquency, op. cit., p. 1.

47. U.S. President, *Manpower Report of the President—March, 1973* (Washington, D.C.: Government Printing Office, 1973), Table C-1, p. 188.

48. U.S. Department of Labor, Bureau of Labor Statistics, *Monthly Labor Review*, 96 (May 1973): Table 15, p. 88.

49. See Ibid.

50. See Doeringer and Piore, op. cit., passim.

51. These concepts are elaborated in Bennett Harrison, "Public Employment and the Theory of the Dual Economy," in *The Political Economy of Public Service Employment* Harold L. Sheppard, Bennett Harrison, and William J. Spring, eds. (Lexington, Mass.: Heath, 1972), pp. 45-55; Barry Bluestone, "The Tripartite Economy: Labor Markets and the Working Poor," *Poverty and Human Resources*, 6 (July-August 1970): 15-35.

52. Authur A. Sloane and Fred Witney, *Labor Relations*, 2d ed. (Englewood Cliffs, N.J.: Prentice-Hall, 1972), p. 220.

53. See Neil W. Chamberlain and James W. Kuhn, *Collective Bargaining*, 2d ed. (New York: McGraw-Hill, 1965), esp. Ch. 3, 8, 9.

54. This is not to deny, however, that, as in all organizations, informal authority and reward systems operate in total institutions. See, for example, Gresham M. Sykes, "The Corruption of Authority and Rehabilitation," *Social Forces*, 34 (1956): 257-62.

Goffman notes that, in total institutions, there exists a system of *secondary adjustments*, defined as "technics which do not directly challenge staff management but which allow inmates to obtain disallowed satisfactions or allowed ones by disallowed means." Erving Goffman, "The Characteristics of

Total Institutions," *Symposium on Preventive and Social Psychiatry* (Washington, D.C.: Walter Reed Army Institute of Research, April 1957), p. 16.

55. On the problems of the role of staff in total institutions, see Sykes, op. cit., pp. 257-62; Goffman, op. cit., p. 16.

56. Board of Trustees, National Council on Crime and Delinquency, op. cit., p. 1.

57. Ibid.

58. Interestingly, the dual labor market theory has recently been more fully developed to include within the primary sector an upper and lower tier. This seems to render the secondary sector a tertiary market along the lines posited in the present analysis. See Michael J. Piore, *Notes for a Theory of Labor Market Stratification* MIT Working Paper, Department of Economics, No. 95 (October 1972).

CHAPTER

4

PUBLIC OCCUPATIONAL
TRAINING AND LABOR
MARKET INFORMATION

Institutions offering occupational training, particularly vocational high schools, have been criticized frequently for their curricula. Specifically, the programs have been found wanting in two respects: first, the course offerings are skewed toward occupations that are not in high demand; second, often the skills taught do not correspond to those required of workers in the "real" world. Consequently, graduates have difficulty finding a training-related position and must accept wages lower than both they and their trainers anticipated. Although researchers debate the methodological issues surrounding the studies that establish these points, there is a general consensus among evaluators and administrators that these shortcomings are pervasive.[1]

The recommendation that logically flows from this criticism is for improvement in planning for occupational training so that offerings will be more closely related to labor market requirements. It is recognized that improved labor market information is required, but the precise type of information necessary, the methods for distributing it, and the mechanism for incorporating such information into programmatic decision making are seldom specified. The purpose of this chapter is to explore the extent to which labor market information is now used in the planning of public training programs in New York City and to assess the potential for enhancing the effectiveness of these programs through an improved labor market information system.

OCCUPATIONAL TRAINING AGENCIES

Occupational training can take place in a variety of settings. Public programs, such as high schools, community colleges, and special adult training efforts are the most important, and they are the primary subject of this

76

chapter. However, it is necessary to note that there are many other programs in operation—notably employer sponsored training, joint union-management apprenticeships, and post-secondary private training schools. Apprenticeships in the New York metropolitan area number about 13,000, with the majority concentrated in construction and printing trades. In New York City there are more than 50 private business schools, teaching various secretarial and other commercial skills. In addition, the State Education Department has licensed 112 private trade schools located in the city, offering courses in fields other than business. The most numerous schools are those for beauty culture, barbering, drafting, and skills for assisting in medical offices, but New York is also the home of the Swedish Institute, which trains masseurs, the Egani Neon Glass Blowing School, and many other unique private institutions.[2]

There are three types of public agencies engaged in occupational training in New York City: agencies in high schools, under the jurisdiction of the Board of Education; those in colleges, particularly community colleges, operated by the Board of Higher Education; and other public programs primarily designed as remedial efforts for adults, which are under the purview of the Manpower Area Planning Council (MAPC).

In the fall of 1970 New York City's high school level population (grades 9 to 12) totalled 426,805. Of this group 92,468 (22 percent) were enrolled in private schools; those in public schools included 49,109 ninth graders in junior high schools, 39,111 vocational high school students, and 246,117 academic high school students.[3] Thus, 9.2 percent of the high school level population in New York City is enrolled in public vocational high schools.

However, a consideration of vocational high school enrollments alone leads to a significant underestimation of the role of occupational training in secondary education. As is evident from Table 4.1, which shows for 1971 the number of graduates, by type of diploma, from public high schools in New York City, many students in academic high schools follow vocationally-oriented curricula. In addition to the 5,234 vocational high school graduates, there were 3,356 academic high school graduates who received commercial or technical diplomas—indicating that they followed vocationally oriented programs. In total, about 21 percent of the public high school graduates received vocational, technical, or commercial diplomas. Moreover, an additional group, probably numbering at least 10,000, received academic or general diplomas but also completed one or more courses that provide occupational skills, such as typing, stenography, or industrial arts.[4]

The difficulties encountered in deriving even a rough estimate of the number of high school students in occupational training programs raises a fundamental point about the employability of youth leaving school. The specific skills acquired in occupationally-oriented courses, whether at a vocational or academic high school, are only one aspect of a youth's employability, because for most entry-level occupations employers attach greater significance to general characteristics, such as appearance, attitudes, and attendance patterns. To the extent that all schooling is intended to develop positive work habits and attitudes, it is appropriate to view all types of high school curricula as enhancing a student's employability, should he choose to enter the labor market upon graduation.

TABLE 4.1

Graduates of New York City High Schools, June 1971

Diploma	Number	Percent
Academic high schools	35,851	100.0
Academic	18,794	52.4
General	13,701	38.2
Commercial	2,466	6.9
Vocational	—	—
Technical and other	890	2.5
Vocational high schools	5,234	100.0
Academic	—	—
General	—	—
Commercial	970	18.5
Vocational	3,997	76.4
Technical and other	267	5.1
All high schools combined	41,085	100.0
Academic	18,794	45.7
General	13,701	33.3
Commercial	3,436	8.4
Vocational	3,997	9.7
Technical and other	1,157	2.8

Sources: Unpublished figures supplied by the Bureau of Educational Program Research and Statistics, New York City Board of Education, and the Information Center on Education, New York State Education Department.

With this caveat in mind, we can examine the fields in which students at vocational high schools are enrolled (Table 4.2). The approximately 70 separate course sequences in the vocational schools may be assigned to 18 major trade categories. The five largest categories—business and clerical, transportation, construction, health, and fashion—accounted for 60 percent of the enrollment in 1970. The largest group (5,389) is in the business fields of secretarial, clerical, and accounting practices. The transportation field (5,009) includes programs in auto mechanics, aviation mechanics, and maritime occupations. Construction (2,926) includes programs in electrical installation, carpentry, and plumbing. The health fields (2,760) are hospital, physician and dental assisting, practical nursing, and dental laboratory processing. The fashion trades (2,219) are primarily manufacturing (that is, sewing), and merchandising and design. The 13 remaining categories, involving approximately 40 percent of the students, are listed in Table 4.2.

TABLE 4.2

Enrollment by Trade Area of Tenth- through Twelfth-Grade Students at Vocational High Schools, 1960 and 1970

Trade Area	1960			1970		
	Number	Percent	Female	Number	Percent	Female
Business and clerical	4,803	14.0	91.5	5,384	17.5	92.0
Transportation	5,792	16.9	0.0	5,009	16.3	0.0
Construction	2,981	8.7	0.0	2,926	9.5	0.0
Health	2,717	7.9	96.9	2,760	9.0	95.8
Fashion	2,462	7.2	84.2	2,219	7.2	91.8
Technical	1,422	4.1	9.1	2,093	6.8	0.0
Cosmetology	2,884	8.4	96.9	1,640	5.3	99.4
Commercial arts	1,397	4.1	28.3	1,639	5.3	41.1
Electronics	1,551	4.5	0.0	1,454	4.7	0.0
Printing	1,668	4.9	0.0	1,340	4.4	0.2
Furniture and woodworking	2,030	5.9	0.0	1,302	4.2	0.0
Distributive	789	2.3	82.6	1,189	3.9	92.5
Metal working	1,578	4.6	0.0	617	2.0	0.0
Electrical and mechanical	284	0.8	0.0	525	1.7	0.0
Miscellaneous	918	2.7	58.9	302	1.0	10.9
Food	752	2.2	13.6	266	0.9	0.0
Drafting	296	0.9	1.0	62	0.2	0.0
Computer	0	0.0	0.0	39	0.1	0.0
Total	34,324	100.0	38.4	30,766	100.0	41.9

Source: Unpublished data supplied by Office of High Schools, New York City Board of Education.

Vocational high school enrollments declined by about 10 percent over the decade of the 1960s, but there were variations from this trend in individual fields.* Seven trade areas experienced expanding enrollment, with the largest gains found in business, technical, and distributive programs. The greatest declines were in cosmetology, metal work, and transportation. Although there were some significant changes in individual programs, the general picture in vocational high schools is one of relative stability. Only one new program area (computers) was introduced, and the five largest fields in 1960 were also the five largest in 1970, accounting for 55 and 60 percent of the total enrollment in each year respectively.

Trade areas in the high schools appear to be highly segregated on the basis of sex. In 10 of the 18 fields no females were enrolled, and in printing only .2 percent of the students were female; in five fields more than 92 percent of the students were female. Aside from the miscellaneous group, only one field— commercial arts— had a relatively even mix of males and females, but this program includes only 5 percent of total vocational school enrollment.

Like the secondary school level, higher education is composed of public and private sectors. In the fall of 1970 there were 358,258 degree credit students, both matriculated and nonmatriculated, enrolled in institutions in New York City.[5] Of this group, 65,695 were at community colleges and technical institutes; 203,652 were undergraduates at senior colleges or universities; 77,918 were graduate students; 10,993 were in first professional programs, such as medical schools and law schools. Among the two-year students, fully 93 percent were in public institutions, primarily the community colleges of the City University of New York (CUNY). Undergraduates at four-year institutions were divided almost evenly between public institutions (53 percent), primarily the senior colleges of CUNY, and approximately 40 private institutions. Graduate students are more heavily concentrated in the private sector (66 percent), primarily the large universities, but it is noteworthy that nearly 27,000 graduate students attend public institutions. First professional students are found almost exclusively in private schools (91 percent), except for those at the Downstate Medical School.

The occupational orientation of programs at the CUNY community colleges is summarized in Table 4.3, which contains data for full- and part-time matriculated students in these institutions.† About half the students (51 percent) were in programs intended to qualify them for subsequent transfer to a senior college; the other half were in career-oriented programs intended to qualify them for skilled jobs upon completion of a two-year program. The

---

*The decline of 10 percent refers to students in vocational programs at the tenth to twelfth grade level. Total vocational high school enrollment actually declined only 2 percent because there was an increase in the number of ninth graders in vocational high schools rather than in junior high schools. The statistics for grades 10 to 12 are more meaningful because they are not affected by reorganizations and because most ninth graders are in exploratory programs rather than in specific vocational courses.

†The total figures in the preceding paragraph and those in Table 4.3 differ because the former include all students while the latter includes only matriculated students.

TABLE 4.3

Matriculated Students at CUNY Community
Colleges, by Field, Fall 1970

	Number	Percent
Transfer students	18,403	50.7
Career students	17,914	49.3
Health	5,039	13.9
Electrician and mechanical technician	2,305	6.3
Accounting	2,138	5.9
Secretarial studies	2,083	5.7
Data processing	1,394	3.8
Business administration and management	1,356	3.7
Marketing	1,029	2.8
Chemical, civil, technical, and drafting	1,013	2.8
Public services	813	2.2
Commercial art	744	2.0
Total, all students	36,317	100.0

Note: Figures may not add due to rounding.

Source: Fall Semester, 1970, Enrollment Report, City University of New York, Department of Budget and Planning, Table X, p. 14.

career group includes students in 37 separate curricula that we have grouped into ten broad areas. The largest area, health-related occupations (5,039 students), includes nursing, dental hygiene, opthalmic dispensing, and several others. Electrical and mechanical technology programs make up the second largest group (2,305). Accounting is a single curriculum with 2,138 students; secretarial studies is another separate program with 2,083 students. Other large fields include data processing, business administration, and marketing.

The community college system has emerged largely during the last decade. The fall 1970 figures include seven CUNY community colleges; by 1973 two more of these colleges had opened. In contrast, only two community colleges existed in 1960, and they enrolled fewer than 7,800 matriculated and non-matriculated degree credit students. The obvious point is that the community colleges have grown rapidly, and many career programs have been introduced in recent years.

Undergraduate education at the bachelor's level traditionally has the least specific vocational orientation. This is reflected in the distribution of degrees granted during 1970-71 (Table 4.4). The two largest fields, social sciences and humanities and fine arts, together account for more than half of all bachelor's degrees (53 percent). Two other important areas are education (12 percent)

TABLE 4.4

Bachelor's and First Professional Degrees Granted by Colleges and Universities in New York City, 1960-61 and 1970-71

Degree and Area	1960-61		1970-71		1960-70
	Number	Percent	Number	Percent	Percent
Undergraduate					
Biological Sciences	789	4.7	1,010	3.5	+ 28.0
Business and Commerce	2,628	15.5	3,449	12.1	+ 31.2
Education	2,281	13.5	3,426	12.0	+ 50.2
English, architecture, mathematics, and science	2,274	13.4	3,222	11.3	+ 41.7
Health	664	3.9	889	3.1	+ 33.9
Humanities and Fine Arts	3,165	18.7	6,277	22.0	+ 98.3
Physical Sciences	944	5.6	818	2.9	- 13.4
Social Sciences	3,995	23.6	8,786	30.8	+119.9
Broad general curricula and miscellaneous	218	1.3	635	2.2	+191.3
Total	16,958	100.0	28,512	100.0	+ 68.1
First professional					
Health	896	36.7	1,068	34.8	+ 19.2
Law	1,357	55.6	1,485	48.3	+ 9.4
Religion	186	7.6	520	16.9	+179.6
Total	2,439	100.0	3,073	100.0	+ 26.0

Sources: Office of Education, U.S. Department of Health, Education and Welfare, *Earned Degrees Conferred, 1960-61*, Report No. OE-54013-61, and unpublished data supplied by the U.S. Department of HEW.

and business (12 percent). Undergraduate education has expanded significantly over the past decade, with degrees rising by 68 percent—that is, from 16,958 in 1960 to 28,512 in 1970. Social sciences and fine arts grew most rapidly, although all other fields, except for the physical sciences, have increased their output.

Professional education in medicine, dentistry, law, and theology produced 3,073 graduates in 1970-71. About half are in law, one-third in health, and the remainder in religion. Each of the professional fields had a greater number of graduates in 1970-71 than in 1960-61, with the total number of degrees up 26 percent.

Graduate education in New York City involves over 65,000 students, with nearly one-third of this group seeking degrees in education (Table 4.5). Other areas with substantial numbers of students are social sciences, humanities, fine arts, and business. Every field, except for the physical sciences, added significant numbers of students over the decade, with the most rapid growth occurring in health (notably hospital administration and pharmacy) and education.

In addition to high school, college, and graduate education, New York City provides its residents with training opportunities through public manpower programs. In fiscal 1971 an estimated 122,936 individuals enrolled in these programs. Their organizational structure is an administrative nightmare, described by the Economic Development Council of New York City as "a fragmented, disjointed, over-lapping conglomerate which did not develop as the result of an overall systematic plan with careful delineation of substantive areas and rational division of administrative responsibility."[6] The New York Manpower Area Planning Council, an agency seeking to coordinate manpower programs, has divided the programs into three categories: prevocational training, public sector employment and training, and training for private sector jobs (Table 4.6). The largest group, accounting for more than half the trainee vacancies ("slots"), is that of public sector programs, consisting primarily of 48,000 summer jobs for teenagers. Training for private sector jobs is divided among the Job Opportunities in the Business Sector (JOBS) program administered by the local Urban Coalition, the Work Incentive (WIN) program for welfare recipients operated by the New York State Department of Labor, the city's Manpower and Career Development Agency (MCDA), which operates its own training centers, training under the federal Manpower Development and Training Act (MDTA) administered primarily by the Board of Education, and several other smaller programs. Prevocational training or basic education is provided under MDTA, by MCDA, and in several other basic education programs.

Specific occupational breakdowns are not available for all programs. Obviously, basic education, which includes nearly one out of every five slots, is not directed towards any specific occupation, but is essential for most. The Neighborhood Youth Corps provides little in the way of training and is primarily a work experience and income transfer program. The Emergency Employment Act has been used to fund numerous jobs in education and health, with fewer positions in other areas. Among public programs geared to private-sector jobs, 40 percent of the slots were for clerical and sales positions, about 15 percent apiece in service occupations (primarily health) and

TABLE 4.5

Enrollment for Advanced Degrees
(Excluding First Professional Degrees) at Universities,
1960-61 and 1970-71

Area	1960-61		1970-71		1960-70
	Number	Percent	Number	Percent	Percent
Biological Sciences	1,049	2.8	1,501	2.3	+ 43.1
Business and Commerce	5,122	13.8	8,695	13.3	+ 69.8
Education	8,934	24.0	20,121	30.8	+125.2
English, architecture, and mathematics	5,606	15.1	7,349	11.2	+ 31.1
Health	343	0.9	888	1.4	+158.9
Humanities and Fine Arts	5,466	14.7	9,786	15.0	+ 79.0
Physical Sciences	1,804	4.8	1,527	2.3	− 15.4
Social Sciences	8,593	23.1	13,243	20.3	+ 54.1
Broad general curricula and miscellaneous	282	0.8	2,276	3.5	+707.1
Total	37,199	100.0	65,386	100.0	+ 75.8

Sources: Office of Education, U.S. Department of Health, Education and Welfare, *Enrollment for Advanced Degrees, Fall 1960;* Report No. OE-54019-60, and *Students Enrolled for Advanced Degrees, Fall 1970,* Report No. OE-72-31.

TABLE 4.6

Training Opportunities in Public Manpower Programs in New York City, FY 1970/71

	Number	Percent
Training for private sector jobs	35,890	29.2
Job Opportunities in Business Sector (JOBS)	7,000	5.7
JOB Optional Program (JOP)	2,250	1.8
MDTA, on-the-job training	3,100	2.5
MDTA, institutional training	3,800	3.1
Concentrated Employment Program (CEP)	714	0.6
Work Incentive program (WIN)	9,600	7.8
Model Cities	800	0.7
MCDA	8,626	7.0
Public sector employment and training	64,255	52.2
Full-time jobs	*3,860*	*3.1*
New careers and public service careers	1,100	0.9
Public Employment program (EEA)	2,020	1.6
Board of Education teacher's assistant	740	0.6
Part-time and summer jobs	*60,395*	*49.1*
Board of Education cooperative education	7,000	5.7
In-school Neighborhood Youth Corps	3,445	2.8
Out-of-school Neighborhood Youth Corps	1,950	1.6
Summer Neighborhood Youth Corps	48,000	39.0
Prevocational and basic education	*22,791*	*18.6*
MDTA, institutional	4,250	3.5
MCDA	3,880	3.2
Concentrated employment program	648	0.5
New careers	1,013	0.8
Adult basic education	6,000	4.9
Welfare education plan	7,000	5.7
Total all programs	122,936	100.0

Source: New York City Manpower Area Planning Council, *Comprehensive Manpower Plan for New York City, Fiscal Year 1973*, pp. 17-18.

processing jobs, and the remainder were allocated among paraprofessionals, machine trades, structural work, and others.[7]

In sum, education and training in New York City in 1970-71 involved 426,805 high school students, 358,258 students at institutions of higher education, and 122,936 manpower program enrollees. While these figures exclude private trade schools and also include among high school students some Neighborhood Youth Corps enrollees, a reasonable estimate is that approximately 850,000 individuals are directly affected by decisions made regarding the nature of curricula at these institutions and programs. We will now consider the extent to which these decisions are informed by current and projected labor market conditions.

LABOR MARKET INFORMATION: DESIRABLE AND AVAILABLE

Somers has outlined the types of labor market information that, "A conscientious vocational educator, charged with the task of planning his course and program offerings for the next few years, would reasonably like to have."[8] His outline can be applied to New York City institutions.

With respect to demand, the basic information requirements are listings of current job openings to assist in placement of graduates and projections of occupational vacancies that correspond in time ranges to the lead time for training programs, to aid enrollment decisions. In order to facilitate the design-of-course content, both current and projected occupational vacancies should specify the skills that applicants are expected to acquire in school versus those acquired on the job. Corresponding data are desirable for labor supply—that is, for each occupation, projections of the output of training programs and the projected supply available through net migration, upgrading of current employees, hiring of trained but unemployed workers, and the utilization of qualified workers outside the labor force, who might return or be enticed to return to the labor force. In brief, to relate training efforts to labor market conditions, comprehensive data on current and projected supply and demand in local areas for specific occupations are required. The success of existing sources of labor market information in meeting these requirements varies according to the types of data—current vacancies, occupational projections, specifications of skill requirements, and supply projections.

As most students of U.S. labor markets know, there is no comprehensive list of job vacancies on a national or local scale. However, rather than seeking knowledge of all vacancies, placement officers seek vacancies appropriate to the number of program graduates. One significant source of vacancy data is the New York State Employment Service (NYSES), which has a network of more than two dozen offices in New York City, and is likely on a typical day to have about 10,500 vacancies listed with its placement office. These vacancies are made available to graduates through NYSES officers assigned to the high schools. Additional vacancies might be listed with the Neighborhood Manpower Service Centers operated by MCDA, which has offices in a number of low-income neighborhoods but does not assign workers to the schools. Private agencies, too, have vacancy listings, but, for obvious reasons these are not made available to school officials.

In addition to employment services, job vacancies can be located through newspaper listings, notably those of the *New York Times*, and through informal contacts, including not only friends and relatives of graduating job seekers but also personal acquaintances of school officials who act on behalf of students. Interviews with faculty and placement officers at several vocational high schools revealed that they often regard employer contacts developed during their own work history as the most important source of placements for students. Department chairmen contact or are contacted by employers with whom they have developed informal relations. In areas that are highly unionized, teachers frequently retain their union membership acquired during previous work experience, using it as a mechanism to help students enter the union.

Ad hoc relationships between school and industry have been formalized through the establishment of an advisory council and advisory commissions. The Board of Education created the 15-member Advisory Council for Occupational Education, including representatives of employers, unions, and academia, which has 45 advisory commissions under it, with a total of almost 1,000 volunteer members. The commissions are organized to provide information on specific fields (industry commissions) and to specific schools (school commissions). While the commissions differ in their activities, all sometimes provide a formal access route to employer representatives that school officials can use to assist in student placement.

Contacts with employers are extended beyond formal and informal links through special job development efforts. School placement officers, as well as job developers at the central Board of Education, approach employers to develop new listings. For their efforts industry- or trade-specific listings of firms, including addresses and phone numbers, are important pieces of information. The most complete listing of businesses in New York City is kept by the New York State Employment Service in its file of firms covered by Unemployment Insurance. The listing, which includes the name, address, number of employees, and industrial activity (by SIC code) of each firm, is used as an internal record-keeping document and has not been distributed to other agencies. The master credit rating file of Dun and Bradstreet Company has similar data but omits many of the smaller firms in the UI list. Dun and Bradstreet has made its file (exclusive of financial data) available to the New York City Planning Commission. This fact became known to job developers at the Board of Education, specifically the Bureau of Cooperative Education, serendipitously. Subsequently, firm names and addresses were made available to the bureau for job-development purposes. Other less complete, but still valuable, employer listings are the commercial telephone directory and various business and trade-association directories.

Occupational vacancy projections are the second type of information used for educational planning. The calculation of future vacancies requires a projection of employment levels; vacancies are then a function of employment change and replacement needs due to retirements, deaths, and so on. Comprehensive projections of employment levels and occupational vacancies have been prepared on a national level by the Bureau of Labor Statistics (BLS) and published as *Occupational Employment Patterns for 1960 and 1975, The U.S. Economy in 1980, Tomorrow's Manpower Needs*, and *Occupational Manpower and Training Needs*.[9] The last document contains projections of annual requirements (growth and replacement needs) for more than 200 specific occupations for the period 1968-80. Special reports dealing in greater detail with manpower requirements for technicians and health also have been prepared and published by BLS.[10]

The BLS projections deal with the nation as a whole, but the bureau's efforts provide a basis for calculating local labor market requirements. Making certain assumptions about the relationships between local and state and state and national employment levels, it is possible to compute projections for New York State and New York City from the national figures. The New York State Department of Labor has undertaken this task and produced in 1968 a set of projections covering 1965-75 and in 1971 revisions covering 1968-80.[11] In each case the number of jobs to be filled (growth plus replacement) in New York City is specified for over 150 occupations. In addition to these comprehensive projections, the state Department of Labor has also prepared detailed studies of selected specialized fields. Other agencies, both public and private, have also prepared surveys and projections in areas, such as health and clerical manpower.[12]

In many respects these reports provide the occupational vacancy projections required for educational planning. Occupational needs for local labor markets are prepared, published and distributed by public agencies. Most officials at the Board of Education, Board of Higher Education, Manpower Area Planning Council, and other training agencies are aware of the data sources and, in fact, generally have copies of the reports in their offices. However, for a variety of reasons, the data are not given great weight in decision making; the most important reasons, which do not relate to the quality of the data, are discussed in the next section of this chapter.

However, educators do raise several criticisms of the occupational projections that should be noted. Most educational administrators are skeptical about the accuracy of the projections. The skepticism is well-founded and merely indicates they take seriously the warning that precedes each of the official sets of figures: "The data should be used as indicators of probable directions and relationships rather than as forecasts."[13] The reason for caution in using projections is illustrated in Table 4.7, which compares employment projections for 1970 based on 1965 data with actual annual averages for 1970. Although the projected total for nonagricultural employment was off by only 46.7 thousand jobs, this net total masks deviations of nearly 297 thousand jobs for the various specific industries. In general the projections underestimate the magnitude of declines in the manufacturing sector and of growth in certain white-collar fields. For example, the projection underestimated by 18.6 thousand, or about 10 percent, the employment decline in the apparel industry, and underestimated by 33.3 thousand, or 22 percent, the growth in banking jobs. Employment growth in communications was underestimated by nearly 20 percent, and in local government by 16 percent.

Netzer's reexamination of Vernon's projections made in the late 1950s, as part of the well-known New York Metropolitan Region Study conducted by Harvard's Graduate School of Public Administration, found similar problems.[14] Vernon projected that white-collar jobs would increase by about 75,000 between 1956 and 1965; the actual increase was about 240,000—and that was before the office boom of the late 1960s! Vernon also projected a minimal increase in government employment, but the number has risen sharply. The higher-than-anticipated growth rates in these fields contrast with faster-than-predicted declines in manufacturing. Over the 1956-65 period New York

City lost nearly 100,000 manufacturing jobs; Vernon projected a modest increase. The combined effect of these miscalculations made Vernon's projections relatively inaccurate. As Netzer concluded, "The total increase in employment in New York City between the mid 1950's and 1965 has been nearly twice as large as the modest increase that was projected."[15]

In addition to being reluctant to trust the accuracy of projections, educators sometimes criticize the occupational classifications used. The BLS and state Department of Labor job categories, formed by merging classifications developed by the Bureau of the Census with those in the U.S. Department of Labor's *Dictionary of Occupational Titles*, do not always correspond to the occupations to which training efforts are oriented. In some cases courses cover a wider range of jobs than those specified in the projections, and in other cases the projections are not of sufficient detail to correspond to individual training programs.

Because of the problems surrounding formal projections, other sources of information are frequently used as indicators of future demand. Most of these sources relate to current labor market conditions. Since projections themselves are extrapolations of current trends, many administrators examine the current situation and make their own judgment about future prospects. The type of current information used for this purpose differs from the current job opening data used for placement purposes. Rather than specific firm names and addresses, general information on the balance between supply and demand is sought.

Unstructured interviews with vocational educators reveal that the informal reports and impressions administrators receive from their placement officers, employer friends, and the newspapers are of greater importance than any formal surveys or statistics on current conditions. When pressed to name a document, administrators frequently select the bimonthly listing, "Occupational Shortages and Surpluses," issued by the New York City office of the New York State Employment Service (NYSES). This short report describes the occupations for which the NYSES has trouble finding qualified applicants and those for which they have a surplus of applicants.

Since replacement needs are an important component of occupational requirements, the total size of an industry or field is one indicator of future demand, and some administrators simply refer to employment statistics reported regularly in state and federal Department of Labor publications and presented periodically in pamphlets prepared by the Regional Office of the Bureau of Labor Statistics.* The joint federal-state Job Vacancies and Labor Turnover Survey (JOLTS) program uses a mail questionnaire to obtain vacancy

---

*The New York State Department of Labor issues *Employment Review, Operations, Manpower Trends,* and *Manpower Review* monthly. The U.S. Department of Labor issues *Monthly Labor Review* and *Employment and Earnings* monthly, and revises *Employment and Earnings in States and Areas* annually. The Regional Office of BLS usually issues an annual "Year-End Report on Jobs, Prices and Earnings in the New York Area," as well as other special bulletins. All these reports contain the same basic data on employment by industry for New York City derived from a monthly survey conducted by the state Department of Labor in cooperation with the federal Department of Labor.

TABLE 4.7

Actual and Projected Employment in New York City, by Industry, 1970
(thousands)

	1970 Projected	1970 Actual	Projected Minus Actual	Difference as Percent of Actual
Total nonagricultural	**3,696.9**	**3,743.6**	**-46.7**	**1.2**
Manufacturing	**814.5**	**766.2**	**+48.3**	**6.3**
Durable goods	184.9	177.7	+ 7.2	4.0
Lumber and wood	5.5	5.2	+ .3	5.8
Furniture and fixtures	17.6	16.3	+ 1.3	8.0
Stone, clay, glass	9.0	7.6	+ 1.4	18.4
Primary metal	13.1	12.4	+ .7	5.6
Fabricated metal	35.4	34.8	+ .6	1.7
Nonelectrical machinery	26.6	25.9	+ .7	2.7
Electrical equipment	44.7	45.4	- .7	1.5
Transportation equipment	9.4	8.7	+ .7	8.0
Instruments and related	23.6	20.4	+ 3.2	15.7
Nondurable goods	629.6	588.5	+41.1	7.0
Food and kindred	57.7	56.6	+ 1.1	1.9
Tobacco	2.7	2.9	- .2	6.9
Textiles	32.9	32.2	+ .7	2.2
Apparel and related	222.5	203.9	+18.6	9.1
Paper and allied	26.3	23.9	+ 2.4	10.0
Printing and publishing	124.9	120.8	+ 4.1	3.4

Chemicals and allied	43.6	40.3	+ 3.3	8.2
Petroleum and coal	7.7	7.7	0.0	0.0
Rubber and plastics	12.3	10.6	+ 1.7	16.0
Leather	28.0	26.7	+ 1.3	4.9
Miscellaneous	71.0	62.9	+ 8.1	12.9
Mining	2.8	1.9	+ .9	47.4
Contract construction	117.3	110.0	+ 7.2	6.5
Transportation, communication and utilities	319.7	323.3	− 3.6	1.1
Railroads	19.0	11.5	+ 7.5	65.2
Air transportation	48.9	56.8	− 7.9	13.9
Communication	76.0	94.5	−18.5	19.6
Telephone and telegraph	60.0	78.7	−18.7	23.8
Radio and television	16.0	15.8	+ .2	1.3
Electricity, gas and sanitary	25.8	25.5	+ .3	1.2
All other	150.0	135.0	+15.0	11.1
Wholesale and retail trade	757.4	735.5	+21.9	3.0
Wholesale trade	306.9	302.2	+ 4.7	3.3
Retail trade	450.5	433.5	+17.0	3.9
Building and farm equipment	8.0	7.5	+ .5	6.7
General merchandise	81.5	92.8	− 5.3	5.7
Variety stores	11.2	23.7	−12.5	52.7
Other stores	76.3	69.1	+ 7.2	10.4
Food stores	74.8	68.5	+ 6.3	9.2

(continued)

TABLE 4.7, continued

	1970 Projected	1970 Actual	Projected Minus Actual	Difference as Percent of Actual
Auto dealers and service	22.0	20.9	+ 1.1	5.3
Apparel and accessories	61.0	61.0	0.0	0.0
Furniture and home furnishings	16.3	19.5	- 3.2	16.4
Eating and drinking places	136.2	118.4	+17.8	15.0
Miscellaneous retail	44.7	45.0	- .3	.6
Finance, insurance, and real estate	401.1	459.6	-58.5	12.7
Banking and credit	119.8	153.1	-33.3	21.7
Brokers and investment	72.0	91.3	-19.3	21.1
Insurance	114.4	119.8	- 5.4	4.5
Real estate	94.9	95.4	- .5	.5
Services	747.6	784.2	-36.6	4.7
Motels and lodgings	36.0	29.5	+ 6.5	22.0
Hospitals	99.9	108.3	- 8.4	7.8
All others	611.7	646.4	-34.7	5.4
Government	536.5	562.8	-26.3	5.7
Federal	107.3	107.5	- .2	.2
State	31.2	40.9	- 9.7	23.7
Local	398.0	414.5	-16.5	4.0

Sources: New York State Department of Labor, *Manpower Directions, New York State 1965-1975,* and Bureau of Labor Statistics, *Employment and Earnings States and Areas, 1939-71,* Bulletin 1370-9.

and turnover data from a sample of New York City firms. The data from the survey will be published by the state Department of Labor (in *Employment Review*), but at present the program is still being developed. In the future, JOLTS data might be a readily available indicator of current labor market conditions for specific occupations and industries.

Occupational supply projections are the type of labor market information it is most difficult, perhaps, for an educational planner to locate. This situation stems from the difficulties of projecting labor supply. In any field, workers are recruited from multiple sources, including promotions, the qualified unemployed, labor force returnees, and migrants. Recent graduates from training programs make up only one segment of the labor supply, and the other sources are very difficult to predict. The difficulty of projecting supply is illustrated by the fact that the state Department of Labor, in the comprehensive set of projections mentioned earlier, estimated the 1970 resident New York City labor force at 3,775,000, a figure more than 11 percent above the 1970 census figure of 3,346,000. Moreover, in a large city, such as New York, any one institution or program is likely to represent only a fraction of new graduates, and the planner for each program should be informed of the anticipated output of other programs. Thus, even if one ignores the problems caused by upgrading, migration, and so on, there are data problems relating to new labor force entrants.

Labor supply information for the local labor market is highly fragmented. Prior to 1973 the Board of Education prepared no systematic projections of output from its programs, nor were current data on trade enrollment and graduations published by the board. In April of 1972 an office of Career Education was established within the central office to coordinate occupational programs. The office issued a master plan containing projected enrollments for 1973-77.[16] The Board of Higher Education has issued and revised its *Master Plan* in 1964, 1968, and 1972; this document reports anticipated levels of enrollment in various fields at CUNY, but most projections have become outdated with the earlier-than-anticipated implementation of an open admissions policy. The MAPC prepares estimates of the number of slots available in each occupational caregory for various public training programs on a fiscal year basis, but the large and varying drop-out rates and the uncertainties of the federal appropriation process results in a distorted picture of actual supply. Little or no data is available on the anticipated output of other programs, such as technical schools, employer programs, and private colleges. In sum, there are no comprehensive supply data available for educational planning.

The fragmented and incomplete nature of supply data has important consequences for enrollment decisions. Even if they accept demand projections as accurate, trainers have no basis upon which to judge the adequacy of supply relative to projected demand. Consequently, they act in an informational vacuum when deciding whether to expand their enrollment in a given field. The result is a bias towards expansion, with the implicit assumption that *other* programs will make necessary adjustments. This feeling is evident in the comments of several vocational educators who believed that, even if general market conditions indicated an occupational surplus, their graduates would find jobs.

Information related to the skills students need before they enter an occupation cannot be presented in quantified form similar to demand and supply estimates. The information that supports curriculum content decisions is drawn almost exclusively from informal sources; the single and most important exception is the Board of Education's Occupational Advisory Council and its commissions. The Advisory Council has periodically surveyed the fields for which training is offered in order to make recommendations concerning new skills that should be taught in high-school courses, as well as concerning equipment needs, ancillary training, and employment prospects. Surveys were conducted in 1968 and in 1970; the 1968 study covered 12 trade areas, and the 1970 study covered 16.[17] In each report specific recommendations were made for curriculum changes. For example, the 1970 report recommended that principles of transistorized equipment be included in the automotive repair program and that new Board of Health regulations in the food service program be reviewed. Interestingly, some recommendations were identical in both the 1968 and 1970 reports. For example, the cosmetology section in each year has as its first recommendation "Skills in servicing wigs and other hair products." Similar examples of repeated recommendations exist in many trade areas. In some cases the advice simply went unheeded, while in other instances the commissions continued to make recommendations which had already been implemented.

In order to strengthen curriculum development the Board of Education sponsored in 1969 a large-scale study of employer perceptions of occupational training in six trade areas. The report emerging from this study, *1000 Employers Look at Occupational Education*, made general recommendations for greater employer involvement in curriculum planning, but there has been little follow-up on the recommendations.[18] In addition to this effort, the board has sponsored special studies during the summer, in which teachers visit firms in their trade areas and examine actual skill requirements for entry level jobs.*

While special studies and reports sponsored by the Board and its Advisory Council may provide some guidance, they are not the primary source of information used for curriculum decisions by principles, department chairmen, and instructors. As indicated earlier, most vocational teachers have experience in industry and maintain contacts with the field through friendships and trade publications. They rely most heavily upon these sources in deciding the skills to emphasize most. For example, a staff member of the High School of Fashion Industry indicated that his informal contacts and *Womens' Wear Daily* were sufficient to keep him abreast of the changes in materials and styles that should be considered in decision making regarding supplies or course content, so as to enable students to gain competence in working with new synthetics or new styles. Although most school administrators are aware of the Advisory Council reports, they give greater weight to the opinions of placement officers, instructors, and industry acquaintances concerning the skills required in each field.

---

*During July of 1971 the following reports were prepared. *Survey of Entry Level Jobs in the Aerospace Industries, Analysis of Entry Level Jobs in Printing*, and *Analysis of Entry Level Jobs in the Fashion Industries.*

THE USES OF AVAILABLE LABOR
MARKET INFORMATION

Existing labor market information falls short of planning ideals. Nonetheless, there does exist a substantial body of information relevant to curriculum and enrollment decisions, and one should examine the barriers to its use before recommending additions to the output of data.

The problem of unused data relates primarily to formal rather than to informal labor market information. As already observed, although informal information about job vacancies and skill requirements is relied upon for placement and curriculum decisions, the data presented in formal reports is relied upon by few school or training officials. Most vocational educators are aware of most of the existing surveys and projections, but few assign great importance to them in decision making. While this situation is in part a function of the shortcomings of the data themselves, there are other considerations that are even more important.

First, and perhaps foremost, among the reasons for limited utilization is the conviction held by many educators that current or future labor market conditions should not dictate course offerings. The position was presented by Jacob Kaufman at a conference on occupational data requirements for education planning: "Somehow the whole idea of making projections is contrary to my idea of the role of education, which is to provide the fullest and widest opportunity for each individual to fulfill his own desires and needs."[19] According to this view, the probable availability of a job after graduation should not be the most important determinant of enrollment patterns. Educators feel strongly that schools exist to serve student interests rather than employer needs. For example, if many students want to learn carpentry, schools should not limit enrollment because not all those trained can be assured jobs. Such extreme choices do not arise frequently because student preferences generally take job prospects into account. But the example raises fundamental questions relating to the purposes of education and training, and most educators take the position that individual choices should be given preference over institutional responses to shifts in the labor market. The model that vocational educators support is one in which students choose among a variety of courses on the basis of interest; their choice is not to be dictated or limited by projections of employer needs. Efforts to promote greater coordination between labor market demand conditions and vocational education are destined to be ineffective when they must be executed by people who lack a commitment to the basic objective.

Educators have additional reasons for giving little weight to vacancy projections. Fewer and fewer vocational high school graduates seek employment immediately after graduation. Since implementation of open admissions at CUNY, less than 40 percent of the vocational high school graduates have gone to work full-time after graduation; most go to college. Consequently, vocational education is increasingly viewed as an alternative educational pattern that appeals to students who might drop out of the academic track. Because they have the option of vocational education,

95

they remain in school and qualify for admission to a community or senior college.

Even for those entering the labor market directly after high school, a training related placement is not always judged to be a suitable evaluative criterion. Program administrators feel that training is a life-long investment and that graduates may eventually return to the trade if labor market conditions change. Skills may be transferred to other fields and, most important, the general work-habits and attitudes instilled during training will serve the student, no matter what type of job he secures.

Another limit to the effective use of labor market information is the administrative structure of occupational training programs. Planning is difficult because at each level—high school, undergraduate, graduate, and adult training—decision making is decentralized. New vocational curricula and the extension of existing programs to additional high schools must be approved centrally at the Board of Education, but the enrollment list for each approved vocational program is determined independently at each of the high schools. There are 94 public high schools in New York City and each principal makes his own enrollment decisions based on available space, student demand, and his perceptions of job opportunities. Since vocational programs can be offered at academic as well as vocational high schools, several schools may be involved in determining the system's total enrollment in any one program. For example, no single individual decides that the high schools will train 500 practical nurses; rather, the principal at each school having an approved program calculates his capacity and the total adds to 500. In 1972 the Office of Career Education was established at the central board to coordinate occupational programs, but it has no line authority over individual schools and cannot regulate enrollments directly. The office has developed a comprehensive plan that incorporates some employment projections, but its planning is divorced from operational decision making.

A slightly more centralized form of authority exists within the City University. The university's policy is to maintain an equal balance between career and transfer programs at the community colleges, and new career programs must be approved by the Board of Higher Education. However, enrollment among existing programs is determined by each of the colleges. Since a program may be offered at more than one institution, the total university enrollment in any occupational program is the result of several independent decisions. The picture in higher education is further complicated by the fact that the public sector accounts for only a fraction of total enrollment. The private sector consists of numerous independent institutions, so higher education as a whole is even more atomistic than the CUNY system.

For public manpower programs the MAPC has responsibility for coordinating training efforts. However, the categorical nature of funding for these programs and the complex administrative arrangements that characterize their organization effectively preclude centralized decisions on occupational priorities. To date MAPC has concentrated on allocating funds among alternative manpower services—placement, job creation, training, and so on—and on selecting priority target populations—drop-outs, addicts, welfare recipients, and the like—for the most effective use of their limited resources. Planning the occupational mix for training efforts can only be accomplished after these fundamental decisions are made.

CONCLUSIONS

Our description and analysis of the use of labor market information in planning occupational training in New York City suggests several concluding observations. Numerous studies of job search behavior have found that informal sources of information, such as friends or relatives, are more heavily relied upon than formal sources, such as placement agencies and job banks. This appears to be the case in institutional as well as in individual decision making: officials at all levels of the various occupational training agencies rely more heavily upon information from professional associates and their own experience than upon projections or reports prepared by public or private agencies.

Accurate and comprehensive data relating to present and future labor market conditions are not available to educational planners—and cannot be in an open, dynamic society. There may be room for improvement in projection methodology, but it is doubtful that local demand can be forecast with great accuracy. If greater resources are to be devoted to training-related labor market information, the funds could best be used to develop more comprehensive profiles of the sources of supply in specific fields.

The most significant obstacles to effective use of labor market information are the attitudes of educators and the decentralized administrative responsibility for occupational training. The educational enterprise is run on the assumption that, beyond certain basic skills, students should be given free choice in selecting their curriculum and that enrollment priorities should be guided by student interests rather than by fluctuating market conditions. In the next chapter we consider the implications for labor market information when a school system is operated in accordance with that principle.

NOTES

1. See two recent summaries: Jerome Mass and Ernest Stromsdorfer, "Evaluating Vocational and Technical Education Programs," in *Vocational Education: Today and Tomorrow*, Gerald Somers and J. Kenneth Little, eds. (Madison, Wis.: University of Wisconsin, Center for Studies in Vocational and Technical Education, 1971); David Rogers, "Vocational and Career Education: A Critique and Some New Directions," *Teachers College Record* (May 1973), pp. 471-512.

2. Apprenticeship data are from New York State Department of Labor, Division of Research and Statistics, "Selected New York Apprenticeship Statistics, 1959-1969," Department Memorandum No. 248, April 1970. Licensed private trade schools are listed in Division of Special Occupational Services,

State Education Department, *Directory of Private Trade Schools in New York State*. Material on private business schools was provided by the Bureau of Business Education, State Education Department.

3. Data in this paragraph are unpublished figures supplied by the Bureau of Educational Program Research and Statistics, New York City Board of Education, and the Information Center on Education, New York State Education Department. Since school districts in New York are in various stages of transition (from an 2-4 to a 6-3-3 to a 4-4-4 organizational structure), some ninth graders are enrolled in high schools, and some in junior high schools.

4. This estimate is based on data relating to the number of classes reported in Board of Education of the City of New York, "Long Range Plans for Comprehensive Occupational Education in New York City," pp. 64 ff.

5. Figures in this paragraph are compiled from National Center for Educational Statistics, *Fall Enrollment in Higher Education: 1970*, Supplementary Information, Institutional Data (Washington: Government Printing Office, 1971).

6. Economic Development Council of New York City, "New York City's Publicly Financed Manpower Programs—Structure and Function." (New York: January 1971), p. 2.

7. See New York City Manpower Area Planning Council, *Comprehensive Manpower Plan for New York City*, FY 1973, Appendix 3A, Table 1.

8. Gerald Somers, "The Response of Vocational Education to Labor Market Changes," *Journal of Human Resources*, Vocational Education Supplement, Vol. III, 1968, p. 41.

9. See *Occupational Employment Patterns for 1960 and 1975*, BLS Bulletin No. 1599 (December 1968): *The U.S. Economy in 1980*, BLS Bulletin No. 1673 (1970); *Tomorrow's Manpower Needs*, BLS Bulletin No. 1606, Vols. I-IV (February 1969); Supplement No. 1 (April 1970); Supplement No. 2 (October 1970) and BLS Bulletin No. 1737 (1971); also *Occupational Manpower and Training Needs*, BLS Bulletin No. 1701 (1971).

10. *Technician Manpower: Requirements, Resources and Training Needs*, BLS Bulletin No. 1512 (Washington, D.C.: Government Printing Office, 1966); *Technician Manpower, 1966-80*, BLS Bulletin No. 1639 (Washington, D.C.: Government Printing Office, 1970); and *Health Manpower, 1966-75*, BLS Report No. 323 (Washington, D.C.: Government Printing Office, 1967).

11. See New York State Department of Labor, Division of Research and Statistics, *Manpower Directions, New York State, 1965-1975*, Vols. I and II and Technical Supplement (New York: State Department of Labor, n.d.); *Manpower Requirements, Interim Projections, New York State 1968-1980*, Publication B-185 (New York State Department of Labor, July 1971).

12. See New York State Department of Labor, Division of Research and Statistics, *Manpower in Selected Metal Crafts, New York State*, Parts I and II (1959); *Technical Manpower in New York State*, Vols. I and II (1964); *Manpower Impacts of Electronic Data Processing*, Publication B-171 (1968); *Manpower Impacts of Industrial Technology*, Publication B-172 (1969). Examples of other studies are New York State Department of Labor, Division of Employment, *Manpower Needs in Health Services* (1969); New York State Department of Health, *New York State Hospital Manpower Survey, 1969* (1970); Economic

98

Development Council of New York City, *New York City's Clerical Manpower Requirements and Problems* (1970); New York Department of City Planning, *Clerical Jobs in the Financial Industry in New York City* (1972).

13. *Manpower Directions . . .*, p. iv. Similar statements appear in each of the official projections.

14. Dick Netzer, "New York's Mixed Economy: Ten Years Later," *Public Interest* (Summer 1969): 188-202. Most of the projections appeared in Raymond Vernon, *Metropolis 1985* (Harvard University Press, 1960), and Egar Hoover and Raymond Vernon, *Anatomy of a Metropolis* (Harvard University Press, 1960).

15. Netzer, op. cit., p. 196.

16. Office of Career Education, Board of Education of the City of New York, *Long Range Plans for Comprehensive Occupational Education in New York City*, (New York City: Board of Education, n.d.) Table XV, p. 114.

17. Advisory Board for Vocational and Extension Education, Board of Education, City of New York, *Five Year Projection and Survey of Twelve Major Industries in New York City for Occupational Training Needs at the High School Level* (April 1968), and *Biennial Survey of Major Industries and Businesses in New York City for Which Occupational Training Is Given at the High School Level* (June 1970).

18. Martin Hamburger and Harry Wolfson, *1000 Employers Look at Occupational Education* (New York: Board of Education, July 1969).

19. Jacob Kaufman's comments, in *Occupational Data Requirements for Education Planning: Proceedings of a Conference* Georgianna March, ed. (Madison, Wis.: Center for Studies in Vocational and Technical Education, 1966), p. 22.

5

IMPROVED INFORMATION
FOR STUDENT DECISIONS

The objective of relating occupational training both to student interests and to labor market conditions must be viewed in broad context. For each individual there is a unique path from childhood to full-time employment, which is determined through a series of decisions that an individual makes or that are made for him. A landmark study of the process described it this way:

> The outstanding conclusion from our findings is that occupational choice is a developmental process: it is not a single decision, but a series of decisions made over a period of years. Each step in the process has a meaningful relation to those which precede and follow it.[1]

Of course, there are constraints that limit the range of options from which an individual can choose. Inherited abilities, the social environment that conditions upbringing, and the economic climate that greets a potential worker—all of these shape decision outcomes. In the United States, however, public policy has sought generally to minimize the constraints and to maximize individual freedom. This policy is the basis of the belief held by educators, that planning for occupational training must be guided by student interests; it is also a suitable basis for assessing the potential for improved labor market information in the schools.

EDUCATIONAL DECISIONS

Many of the most important decisions influencing personal development relate to the selection of secondary and post-secondary school curricula. In the pre-school period what a child is taught is determined almost exclusively by his parents. As mandatory school attendance laws take effect almost all children are exposed to the uniform requirements of elementary education. Some may progress more rapidly than others, but for all children the common goal of elementary school remains the "three R's."

Students and their families generally face their first curriculum decision in the junior high or intermediate school. Options are offered in the field of mathematics and foreign languages. Those who have done well in elementary school may be encouraged to take the more challenging courses, while those who experienced difficulty are cautioned against such courses.

More important decisions are made at the end of the eighth or ninth grade, depending upon the type of elementary or junior high school a student attends. At this point a student selects the high school he will attend and his course of study. There are 96 public high schools in New York City; 25 are vocational high schools, 62 are academic high schools and 9 are designated comprehensive high schools.[2] Most of the academic high schools are "zoned"— that is, they accept students from designated areas; the typical pattern is for a student to move from junior high to a zoned high school. At high school he may choose from among a variety of courses. Prior to 1973 his program could lead to an academic, commercial, technical, or general diploma. Since 1973 all students receive a single diploma with the specific courses completed listed on the reverse side. Despite the change in diploma policy, there still exists a wide variety of courses that students may take at academic high schools. Limitations are placed on student choices in certain cases only—for example, several zoned academic high schools have designated programs with special admission requirements; included in this group are certain technical, art, and music majors that are open only to students who pass an admissions test.

Alternatively, a student leaving junior high might choose to enter one of the specialized public high schools. Three schools—Bronx High School of Science, Brooklyn Technical High School, and Stuyvesant High School—have academic programs filled by citywide competitive examinations. Programs at the vocational high schools are divided into those requiring an entrance examination and those open to all applicants. Students may opt for any of the vocational curricula, provided they pass the necessary entrance examination.

Once in high school, the student's most important decision is whether to complete his chosen program. In the last two years of high school, manadatory attendance laws might no longer be applicable, and many individuals leave the educational system. Generally, drop-outs enter the labor market and seek work. Often they encounter great difficulty because of lack of skills and employer bias. Teenage unemployment rates, particularly for blacks and females, are far above the rate for the total labor force. Many youths, not finding regular work, leave the labor force to become involved in the city's numerous illicit activities. One teenager interviewed in a study of slum unemployment put it this way: "I'm just hanging around. If things get too boring during the summer I'll find something to do. . . . This is America, man—you can always make money pushing numbers or something.[3]

The majority of high school students, who do complete the requirements for a diploma, face a critical choice at graduation between work and various educational opportunities. A sizeable minority moves directly into the labor force. Those with general diplomas or poor records can have difficulty finding a job, and their unemployment and labor force participation rates approach those of drop-outs. Others, who are better prepared or have family connections with employers, are likely to find a suitable place for themselves in the city's diverse economy.[4]

The majority of high school graduates move on to another stage of schooling. Some graduates elect to enter private post-secondary training centers that offer courses in secretarial or other skills. The largest group consists of those entering college. Graduates may apply to whatever college they wish, but since 1970 the city's Board of Higher Education guarantees all graduates a place within the City University's network of senior and community colleges. Those entering the City University will be assigned to a college on the basis of their own preference and their high school record. Students are admitted to the college of their choice, if space permits. Where applications exceed capacity, students are selected on the basis of high school average or rank in class, whichever is more favorable, with the special provision that anyone having at least an 80 average or who ranks in the top 50 percent of his class will be admitted to a senior college if he so chooses. Those not meeting one of these standards are admitted to a community college, as are those whose first preference is a community college.

Once in college, a student pursues his chosen major. At community colleges there are about three dozen career programs with an occupational orientation and more than a dozen transfer programs intended to serve as the first two years of a full bachelor's degree curriculum. At the senior colleges there is a full range of four-year majors. Of course, students may decide not to continue their education and leave college before earning a degree. Others may switch between full- and part-time status, taking a longer period to complete their programs, and still others follow the traditional route as full-time students. Eventually most students completing their degrees enter the labor market either directly or via graduate or professional schools.

In sum, there are a number of different educational paths open to youths in New York City. Data will be presented below, describing the actual pattern of decisions in recent years, but it is useful first to consider the information available to students when they make these critical decisions.

INFORMATION FOR STUDENT DECISIONS

Each educational decision is likely to be made after consultation with family and friends. Parents' and peers' knowledge, added to that derived from a student's personal experiences, form a background for decision making; information so acquired is likely to be trusted and well received. But often the family alone cannot provide the young person with the full range of information he desires in making a decision. Parents might know about their alma mater; the child probably weighs their views of the school carefully in selecting his college, but he is likely to want to know about other schools as well.

Friends and relatives provide information about the various occupations in which they are engaged, but an individual might be curious about a field outside the range of their experiences. In order to fill these gaps, educational institutions establish informational services of different types.

In the public schools, information is provided by guidance counselors. The New York City Board of Education reported that in 1971-72 it employed 628 elementary school counselors, 384 junior high school counselors and 222 regular high school counselors.[5] Pupil-counselor ratios vary widely among schools, but the systemwide average for community school districts (elementary and junior high) was 1:840 and the figure for high schools about 1:1,200. The full-time high school counselors are supplemented by a large number of school personnel who spend one or more periods daily serving as grade advisor, college advisor, or in some similar capacity. In addition, there are 160 counselors hired under special federally-funded projects, such as Towards Upward Mobility, College Bound, or College Discovery, that reach about 7 percent of the high school population.

The role of junior high and high school counselors is ambiguous. Principals might expect counselors to serve as their agents, dealing with disruptive problems or other crisis situations, but some counselors feel a professional obligation to deal with students as their clients.[6] Counselors who seek to help their "clients" in making informed decisions need not rely exclusively on their personal experience; the Board of Education prepares the following guidance materials: a *Directory of Public High Schools*, which is available to students to help them select an appropriate secondary school; a *Directory of Adult Education*, which provides a listing of evening and adult programs run by the board; a *College and Career Guide* published for high school students, which describes specific opportunities in higher education and employment; and a bi-weekly memorandum distributed to counselors containing current information on topics, such as scholarship opportunities or job training programs. In addition to board materials, in assisting their college-bound clients counselors generally make use of several privately published directories containing basic data on institutions of higher education; general information describing the nature of various kinds of work are provided in the *Occupational Outlook Handbook* and the *Occupational Outlook Quarterly*, both prepared by the U.S. Department of Labor.[7]

Information and guidance is also made available to college students. The general pattern is for a departmental advisor to help in the selection of courses to assure that all degree requirements are fulfilled. In addition, since the implementation of open admissions at the City University, testing and counseling have been made available to entering freshman to help determine whether they require remedial course work.

Specific information relating to job opportunities for students is provided through the services described in Chapter 4. The key figures are school placement officers, counselors from the New York State Employment Service, personnel in the city's Neighborhood Manpower Service Centers, and representatives from business firms who visit schools and campuses to recruit new workers.

The interaction between family backgrounds and guidance services and educational opportunities in shaping career pathways in New York City is outlined in Figure 5.1. This chart represents an estimate of the relative importance of various decision outcomes for the cohort of students entering the tenth grade in the fall of 1967, which is the first group of students to benefit from the City University's Open Admissions policy. Their choices are particularly significant because their experiences are likely to indicate future trends.[8]

A total of 113, 159 students were enrolled in the tenth grade in the fall of 1967. Of this group 65.7 percent attended public academic high schools, 13.6 percent attended public vocational high schools, and 20.7 percent attended private schools. The proportion of black and Puerto Rican students is approximately 50 percent for the academic high schools, 65 percent for the vocational high schools, and 15 percent for private schools.

During three years of high school a strikingly large number of students drop out. Enrollment figures and the number of diplomas granted are presented in Table 5.1. The estimated noncompletion rate is 44 percent for the academic high schools, 65 percent for the vocational schools, and 53 percent for the public system as a whole. These figures, based on the three-year period beginning in the tenth grade, are in line with overall noncompletion rates estimated at about 40 percent in other studies for the last two years of high

TABLE 5.1

Enrollment and Diplomas for a Cohort of
Tenth Graders in New York City
Public Schools, 1967-70

	Academic Public High Schools	Vocational Public High Schools	All Public High Schools
Tenth grade (fall 1967)	74,324	15,389	89,713
Eleventh grade (fall 1968)	65,352	9,941	75,293
Twelfth grade (fall 1969)	49,640	6,875	56,515
Diplomas (January and June 1970)	41,399	5,326	47,654

Source: Data supplied by New York City Department of City Planning, Educational Planning Section.

FIGURE 5.1

Decision Outcomes for a Cohort of New York City Tenth Graders

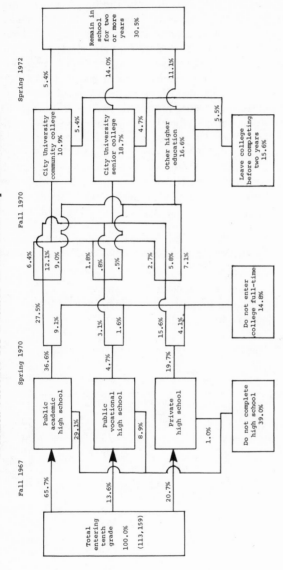

Sources: Figures for tenth-grade enrollment in each type of school and for diplomas (graduates) for public academic and vocational schools were supplied by the Educational Planning Section, New York City Department of City Planning. Nonpublic school graduate data are from Information Center on Education, New York State Education Department. Graduates were allocated to alternative outcomes on the basis of figures reported in Robert Birnbaum and Joseph Goldman, *The Graduates: A Follow-up of New York City High School Graduates of 1970*, (City University of New York, May 1971), various pages. Attrition rates were estimated at 50 percent for community colleges, 25 percent for senior colleges and 33 percent for other higher education based upon figures reported in Office of Institutional Research, Bronx Community College, "Attrition and Student Progress at Bronx Community College, September 1970 to June 1972" (Bronx Community College, January 1973), and David Lavin, "Open Admissions Research at City University of New York," in *Testimony before Joint Legislative Committee on Higher Education* (City University of New York, November 17, 1971), various pages.

105

school.[9] When figures for the private schools are combined with those for the public schools, the total noncompletion rate is estimated to be 39 percent (see Figure 5.1).

Drop-outs are concentrated in the public schools and are disproportionately black and Puerto Rican. About 50 percent of the tenth-grade public school population is white, but the figure rises to about 60 percent in eleventh grade, to two-thirds at the beginning of twelfth grade, and to about 70 percent at graduation. When private school figures are included, 76 percent of all high school graduates in New York City are white.[10]

For the 60 percent who complete high school, college is the dominant choice (Table 5.2). Of this group, 76 percent were attending school full-time the second college year, and an additional 2 percent attended part-time. The 1970 full-time school attendance rates for public academic graduates is 75 percent, for vocational graduates 67 percent, and for private school graduates 79 percent. Prior to 1970 about 59 percent of all graduates continued their schooling; the total figure for 1970 is 76 percent, and for 1971 it is 73 percent. Open Admissions has significantly altered the educational patterns of many graduates, particularly those from vocational schools and those with low grades in academic schools. Many individuals who might have entered the labor market immediately after graduation are now going to college, and the number

TABLE 5.2

Percent of High School Graduates Continuing Education Full Time, New York City, 1970 and 1971

	1970	1971
Total, all graduates	76	73
Public vocational school graduates	67	54
Public academic school graduates	75	74
Private school graduates	79	79
Male graduates	83	76
Female graduates	70	72
White graduates	78	75
Black graduates	67	68
Puerto Rican graduates	63	62
Latin American graduates	67	71
Oriental and other graduates	88	79

Sources: Robert Birnbaum and Joseph Goldman, *The Graduates* (New York: City University, May 1971); Arthur Blank et al., *The Graduates Restudied* (New York: City University, Center for Social Research, September 1972).

of graduates looking for full-time work is relatively small. For the 1970 cohort, fewer than 15 percent entered the pool of full-time workers immediately after graduation.

The City University is the major avenue of higher education in New York City (Table 5.3). Nearly 30 percent of the entire cohort—about 48 percent of all graduates, and 64 percent of all graduates continuing in school—enroll in

TABLE 5.3

Choice of College Among New York City
Graduates Attending College, 1970 and 1971
(in percent)

	1970	1971
All high schools	100.0	100.0
CUNY senior college	40.3	42.7
CUNY community college	23.8	24.5
Private school in N.Y. City	15.9	15.8
Other school in N.Y. State	10.3	11.4
All others	9.7	5.6
Public academic schools	100.0	100.0
CUNY senior college	44.0	47.9
CUNY community college	23.2	23.9
Private school in N.Y. City	11.1	9.8
Other school in N.Y. State	13.6	11.4
All others	8.1	7.0
Public vocational schools	100.0	100.0
CUNY senior college	25.2	39.4
CUNY community college	57.5	39.9
Private school in N.Y. City	12.1	9.6
Other school in N.Y. State	3.6	7.7
All others	1.6	3.4
Private high schools	100.0	100.0
CUNY senior college	36.9	34.8
CUNY community college	17.5	22.3
Private school in N.Y. City	25.6	27.1
Other school in N.Y. State	11.5	11.9
All others	8.5	3.9

Sources: Robert Birnbaum and Joseph Goldman, *The Graduates* (New York: City University, May 1971); Arthur Blank et al., *The Graduates Restudied* (New York: City University, Center for Social Research, September 1972).

one of the university's units. Nearly two of every three graduates going to CUNY attends a senior college rather than a community college.

Open admissions has significantly altered the racial mix on CUNY campuses. While white graduates are still more likely to attend college (78 percent) than blacks (67 percent) or Puerto Ricans (63 percent), the differences are relatively small, and the New York City minority group rates well above the national averages. Moreover, minority graduates are more likely than whites to attend CUNY. Consequently, the entering freshmen class at CUNY shifted from 14 percent black and 6 percent Puerto Rican in 1969 to 20 percent black and 9 percent Puerto Rican in 1971; the number of black and Puerto Rican freshmen tripled in this two-year period.[11]

Comprehensive data are not available on attrition during higher education. However, a study of students admitted to one of the CUNY community colleges in 1970 has recently been completed, and it is reasonable to assume that patterns similar to the one it describes exist at other campuses.[12] Of the total group entering in the fall of 1970, there were 58 percent still registered in the spring of 1972. Some of those no longer in attendance might have transfered to other schools but most probably discontinued their education. However, it is important to add that while 58 percent were still in school that semester, only 7 percent received a degree in June 1972. The remainder (51 percent) were taking longer than expected to earn their degree; some might never graduate, in fact.

Less is known about attrition at CUNY senior colleges. Data for the first year of Open Admissions indicated that 20 percent of the senior college freshmen left within a year. After two years, the figure has probably risen higher than the national average for four-year institutions (23 percent). For New York City high school graduates attending institutions other than units of the CUNY, it is likely that two-year attrition is similar to the national average for all college entrants (33 percent). When these separate attrition rates are combined, it is revealed that while about 46 percent of the cohort enter college, only 30 percent are still there two years later (see Figure 5.1).

The outcomes for the total group can best be summarized by looking at the cohort in terms of the time that members leave the educational system. About 39 percent drop out before finishing high school; 15 percent do not go beyond high school graduation; 16 percent enter college but leave before completing two years; 30 percent remain in school beyond that point. The two important trends behind these figures are a high public school drop-out rate and high college attendance rates among all high school graduates.

IMPLICATIONS FOR INFORMATION SERVICES

The changing trends in educational pathways into the labor market have important implications for the provision of career-related information to students. At each critical decision point, informational needs are changing.

The high rates of college attendance among students in all types of programs make the choice of curriculum in high school less important. The

City University's policies of open admissions and free tuition have made college widely available, and many students in vocational schools who had never considered the possibility in the past are now taking advantage of it. Consequently, the choice of high school courses no longer necessarily forecloses certain options. Since 1970 the majority of vocational high school graduates has been going to college full-time. As other students become increasingly aware of their options, they are likely to be more willing to deviate from the traditional college-preparatory program in their course selections.

The Board of Education's newly implemented (1973) single diploma policy and the creation of comprehensive high schools will contribute even further to the blurring of distinctions in high school programs. Increasingly the selection of courses should be viewed as a matter of alternative ways for students to acquire certain basic skills related to employability and college entrance. The difference between "occupational" and "academic" courses represents a contrast in pedagogical techniques as much as a difference in skills taught. For example, basic principles of science are taught both in the electrical shop and in the physics laboratory; typing is taught both as a secretarial skill and as a practical aid for individuals aspiring to college. One curriculum may be better than another in preparing students for college, but the choice is no longer an irreversible one, and each course provides a choice of future options. Students should be aware of the relative merits of each course, but they should also be encouraged to·explore course offerings that appeal to them, regardless of the educational track in which the course falls.

A high drop-out rate continues to plague the city's public schools. A substantial minority of all tenth graders (39 percent) does not finish high school. The factors that cause students to drop out, such as limited family income, role models, peer pressure, and a fundamental dissatisfaction with the educational process, are difficult to change in the short run. Consequently, the drop-out rate is not likely to be significantly reduced simply through improved informational or guidance services. But students leaving school before graduation should be well informed about the possible consequences of their act and the options that it might close off. As more and more of their peers attend college, the education gap will widen between drop-outs and those who remain in the education system. Drop-outs should be advised of the procedures for returning to school eventually; opportunities for pursuing training in some other setting, such as adult training programs; opportunities for obtaining equivalency diplomas; and employment assistance available from state, city, and private agencies. Although dropping out is a way into the labor market for a substantial number of youths, drop-outs are at present given relatively little attention by schools and employment services.

For those who graduate and seek to enter the labor market, both information services and employment prospects are brighter. The city's large employers recruit high school graduates, and there are school placement officers and representatives of the NYSES available at selected schools to assist in the job search. While continuing efforts should be made to improve such services, the declining number and proportion of graduates entering the labor market should help reduce the employment problems of this group, provided the city's general economy remains healthy.

For graduates who go on to college, the important informational needs relate to deciding on the institution to attend. For the relatively small group going to private or out-of-town schools, the choice is usually made in terms of preferences voiced by family or friends, after a consideration of several options. For most graduates, the choice is between campuses of the City University, and there is room for improving the informational base for this decision making. Freshman enrollment at CUNY now favors senior colleges over community colleges by about two to one. One of the distinguishing characteristics of the CUNY Open Admissions experience as compared to similar systems, notably in California, is that a large share of newly qualified entrants is absorbed by senior colleges. Although this absorption is in part a function of the physical capacity of existing structures and of the desire to keep the campuses racially integrated, it is possible that better information about the variety of programs and transfer opportunities available at community colleges might shift more students towards those institutions.

The group attending college has a drop-out problem approaching in relative importance that of high school students. An increasing number of individuals enter the labor market after a brief college experience rather than immediately after high school. Placement and counseling services for this group could be significantly improved. The need has been recognized by CUNY officials: "Obviously, more extensive counseling is required, with an emphasis on final interview for the student who is definitely leaving, so that the student may be counseled in realistic alternative courses of action within CUNY or elsewhere."[13] The fact that many who stay in school take longer than anticipated to earn their degrees is evidence of the need for better academic counseling to ensure that students are aware of requirements and that they enroll in suitable courses.

Finally, the possibility that the high attrition rates at CUNY may lead to a future decline in college attendance rates should be noted. New cohorts will become aware of the experience of their predecessors through informal contacts and other sources of feedback. If their plans are altered by the unsatisfactory experiences of brothers, sisters, and older friends, college attendance rates may begin to decline. Open admissions and other shifts in educational policy have recently caused dramatic changes in the career paths of New York City youth; there is, however, no assurance that these patterns will remain stable, and informational services should constantly be adjusted to the changing needs of students.

In sum, this review of educational pathways in New York City has identified several key points at which improved information services might help students. High school curriculum decisions should be placed in the context of what best suits an individual's learning style, not as a critical decision that limits future options. Drop-outs should be advised of the options they are foreclosing and informed of alternative training opportunities, reentry routes to an academic track, and employment services available to assist in the transition to work. The increased number of graduates entering college, and particularly the City University system, should be better informed about two-year career programs and the relative merits of senior and community colleges. Those who enter but do not complete college should, like their high school counterparts, be directed to alternative training opportunities and available placement services.

NOTES

1. Eli Ginzberg et al., *Occupational Choice: An Approach to a General Theory* (New York: Columbia University Press, 1951), p. 185.

2. Board of Education of the City of New York, *Long Range Plans for Comprehensive Occupational Education in New York City*, (New York City: Board of Education, n.d.) p. 59.

3. Quoted in Stanley Friedlander and Robert Shick, *Unemployment in the Urban Core*, (New York: Praeger, 1972), p. 174.

4. For an analysis of the ways high school graduates find a place in the world of work see Marcia Freedman, *The Process of Work Establishment*, (New York: Columbia University Press, 1969).

5. Figures in this paragraph are from Board of Education of the City of New York, op. cit., pp. 35-40.

6. See Eli Ginsberg, *Career Guidance*, (New York: McGraw-Hill, 1971), for discussion of the role of counselors.

7. The general information sources available to counselors are described in Willa Norris, Franklin Zeran, and Raymond Hatch, *Information Service in Guidance*, (Chicago: Rand McNally, 1966), particularly Chs. 6 and 7.

8. The Birnbaum and Goldman study, *The Graduates: A Follow-up of New York City High School Graduates of 1970* (New York: City University, May 1971), was replicated for 1971 graduates. See Arthur Blank et al., *The Graduates Restudied: A Comparison of the Follow-up of New York City High School Graduates of 1970 and 1971* (New York: City University, Center for Social Research, September 1972). Figures for both years are shown in Tables 5.2 and 5.3, but 1970 figures were used for constructing Figure 5.1.

9. See Citizens Committee for Children of New York, *A Report on New York City High Schools* (January 5, 1970), and Birnbaum and Goldman, op. cit., pp. 38-41.

10. Birnbaum and Goldman, op. cit., Tables 3-5, 3-6; Bureau of Program Research and Statistics, Board of Education of the City of New York, "Annual Census of School Population, October 30, 1970" (April 1971).

11. Joe L. Rempson, "Minority Access to Higher Education in New York City," *City Almanac*, August 1972.

12. Office of Institutional Research, Bronx Community College, "Attrition and Student Progress at Bronx Community College, September 1970 to June 1972" (Bronx Community College: January 1973).

13. James McGrath, "Effects of Open Admissions on the Operation of CUNY's Colleges," in *Testimony before Joint Legislative Committee on Higher Education*, November 17, 1971, p. 28.

CHAPTER

6

THE MAJOR
LABOR MARKET
INSTITUTIONS IN
NEW YORK CITY

This study will have a somewhat broader focus than the two that preceed it. Whereas in Chapters 2-5 the role of manpower information is examined in reasonably discrete (but complex) areas, in this and the next chapter we explore the somewhat amorphous relationships between information and the major institutions in New York City's labor market—employers, unions, and, in particular, the government of New York City.

As defined by Yavitz and Morse, labor market intermediaries are those institutions that significantly affect the flows and arrivals of direct labor market participants into the specific, narrow market of those seeking and those offering jobs.[1] New York City's Board of Education and Department of Corrections are clearly labor market intermediaries. Though both are primarily concerned with shaping the supply side of the labor market equation, they are also direct participants in the labor market, because they are employers. Indeed, the Board of Education, which employs over 100,000 persons, including part-time employees, is one of New York City's major employers.

The government of New York City, which is the primary subject of inquiry in this study, is the single most important intermediary and the single most important direct participant in the city's labor market. As an intermediary, the city government affects both the demand for and the supply of labor through a number of linkages with the local economy that will be examined later in this chapter. The city government's role as a direct participant is affirmed by the fact that it employs more than 10 percent of the city's job-holders. Businesses and unions also, of course, are intermediaries and direct participants in the local labor market.

If the focus of this study is broad, so too is the concept of information with which we are concerned. Information is viewed as knowledge of any kind about the local economy that is considered relevant for decision-making purposes by employers, unions, and city government. Yavitz and Morse suggest that the proximity of a given intermediary to the specific employer-employee exchange determines in large part the nature of information that is needed by a given intermediary.[2] The more proximate the intermediary is to the specific employer-employee exchange, the greater the intermediary's need for labor market information that is both current and specific; the further removed the intermediary is from the specific job market, the greater is its need for aggregative, long-range information.

In Chapters 2-5 it was clearly indicated how the functioning of intermediaries with respect to the local labor market determines the relevance of various kinds of data. Information relevant to an employment agency or probation officer attempting to effect a single union between an employer and prospective employee is clearly not the same kind of information as that required by the Board of Education attempting to adjust its curriculum to a changing economy. The informational needs of the city government are dramatically inclusive. Of course, when the city government hires employees, its labor market information needs might be akin to the needs of a single corporate employer, but when the city government relates to the local economy in other ways (perhaps, in attempting to stimulate local job development or to develop policies designed to improve reading scores in the public school system), its informational needs are of a very different nature.

This study draws heavily on another conclusion from Yavitz and Morse, that labor market information is "closely related to the character of a city's economic activity."[3] Not only does the existing stock of information seem to be a function of certain labor market characteristics but, as this study indicates, the use of information is also dependent on the character of the local economy. Furthermore, it is strongly suggested in this study that the potential that better labor market information holds for improving labor market efficiency is in very large part a function of local economic, social, and political conditions.

Thus, borrowing from the insights of Yavitz and Morse, the starting point for this study is not with labor market information per se, but with a description of three of the most important actors who use labor market information within the specific context of New York City. In Chapter 7 labor market information in New York City is characterized, its potential significance appraised, and some general observations are made, pertinent to the continuance of research in the area of urban labor market information.

THE PRINCIPAL NONGOVERNMENTAL ACTORS

The most distinguishing characteristic of New York City's economy (and of the city's political and social systems as well) is its complexity. The complex nature of the city's economy is primarily a function of the economy's scale and diversity. Size alone might not make an urban economic system complex, but once an urban economy reaches a sufficient scale, diversification of economic function is a likely concomitant.[4] To an unparalleled degree this has occurred in New York City.

113

The direct and indirect participants in the local labor market are so numerous and the functions they perform so diverse that understanding the way the city's economy functions, let alone communicating that understanding in the form of useful information, is very difficult. Compounding the problem from an informational viewpoint is the fact that the economy is changing rather rapidly. Finally, change produces conflict. Conflict arising from change may be more pronounced generally in the arena of politics than in economics, but, as we will see later, conflict affects the nature, use, and utility of labor market information.

Employing Institutions

The same factors that make the local economy complex—size, diversity, and change—are reflected in the character of the city's employing institutions. The structure of the city's employing institutions not only affects the kinds of labor market information they need but the supply of labor market information that is available to them.

New York City's approximately 225,000 employing institutions, including businesses, nonprofit organizations, and governments, employ 3.54 million persons.[5] The typical business firm in the city employs relatively few persons however,[6] and the average number of employees per employing unit—only about 16—is inflated by the fact that three of the city's employing institutions—the federal, state, and city governments,—employ over 550,000 persons.[7] While it is true that many of the city's employers, in particular the thousands of small "mom and pop" stores that service narrow geographic areas, do not require very much labor market information in the day-to-day conduct of their business, a very large number of diverse businesses do require substantial amounts of information about the economy.

Not only are there more employing institutions in New York City than in any other city, but the diversity of goods and services produced in the city, as well as their volume, is unmatched by any other urban economy in the world. No single activity dominates the city's economy. In terms of employment, the service industry (excluding government) employed more persons by 1970 (22 percent of the total) than manufacturing (20.2 percent). Government (14.7 percent) and finance, insurance, and real estate (12.2 percent ranked third and fourth in employment.[8] In terms of goods and services produced, the city's economy is remarkably diverse, even in the manufacturing sector. Lichtenberg pointed out in 1960 that virtually all of the 446 census classifications of manufactured goods were produced in New York City.[9] The variety of manufactured goods produced locally may be somewhat less today due to the continual decline of manufacturing activity, but the city remains the national center for the production of many items, particularly unstandardized consumer goods. The single largest service provider, the city government, delivers a broader spectrum of services than any other local government in the nation. The private service-providing sector represents, of course, the epitome of diversification of function.

114

Finally, the city's employing institutions are characterized by a rapid rate of change, not only at the level of individual business firms but also between sectors of the economy. While the total number of jobs in New York City increased only moderately during the 1960s, the composition of the city's jobs changed substantially. Heavy losses in the manufacturing sector were more than offset by employment increases in the service sector, particularly in the city government. In addition to substantial intersectoral changes, the city's economy is characterized by a high turnover rate at the individual firm level, particularly among smaller firms. With respect to major corporations the same pattern holds true, though the net loss of major corporations has not been as large as is popularly thought. In 1960 New York City was the corporate headquarters location of 131 of *Fortune's* top 500 firms. Between 1960 and 1971 a total of 27 of these firms moved out of the city, but 15 other firms in the top 500 relocated in the city during the same period. The number of New York City-based firms in the second 500 largest corporations has increased slightly in recent years.[10]

These characteristics—the large number of small employers, the diversity of goods and services produced, and the rapid rate of change in the economy—have important implications for labor market information in New York City. For one thing, groups in a rapidly changing system, particularly one that is marked more by internal change than growth, as is the case with the city's economy, face substantial adaptive challenges. Information, along with several other endogenous resources, such as skilled management and a flexible labor force, is a critical determinant of adaptive capacity. Unfortunately, it might be more difficult to obtain good information in such an environment than in a less fluid system.

In addition, the scope and diversity of labor market information that employers need are such that no information producer, no matter how large, ever could hope to supply even a fraction of the information about the city's economy that employing institutions require. As one might expect, the flow of information to the city's employers is provided by numerous, rather specialized information producers. Businesses in New York City rely heavily on trade associations for information concerning general industrywide conditions and, in many instances, for basic data used in the conduct of collective bargaining.[11] Private firms also employ specialized consulting businesses to provide certain kinds of labor market information.[12] Public employment agencies, such as the New York State Employment Service, compete (in general, poorly) with private employment agencies for the attention of New York City businesses in the field of hiring. The Middle Atlantic Regional Office of the U.S. Bureau of Labor Statistics, perhaps the city's most visible and frequent information producer, commonly provides labor market information to interested employers. A number of prominent business interest groups that cut across industry lines, such as the Economic Development Council, maintain research staffs generally oriented to providing information about the government and economy of New York City.*

---

*Other prominent business interest groups oriented to information production include the New York Chamber of Commerce and Industry and the Citizens Budget Commission.

In Chapter 7 some of the qualitative weaknesses in the city's information base are discussed. With respect to the city's private employing institutions, it would appear that, on balance, adequate labor market information exists for many corporate purposes; when this is not the case, most major corporate employers who need information—for example, for long range planning purposes—are usually able to generate that information, either internally or by acquiring it from external sources.

Unions

Since labor unions represent people who work for employing institutions, union organization tends to reflect the nature of the labor force and the structure of industry in any given economic system. The union movement in New York City inherits certain strengths and weaknesses from the city's labor market.

The most obvious strength of the city's union movement is the size of its membership. In addition to the approximately 1.4 million union members who work in the private sector, there are some 300,000 unionized public employees, most of whom are employees of the city government. Thus, about half of the city's total workforce of slightly more than 3.5 million persons is made up of union members.

The union movement in New York City is also extremely diverse. Again, this is a function of local economic and labor force characteristics. No single union or union leader dominates the city's labor movement, though the building trades unions remain the most influential group.* Other large and influential organized employee groups include building service employees, garment workers, longshoremen, transportation workers, retail employees, taxi drivers, hospital workers, and, in the public sector, teachers, transit workers, police, firemen, and clerical employees.

What formal intergroup cohesion exists in the city's labor movement is provided by the Central Trades and Labor Council, a body of delegates from about 700 of the city's roughly 1,000 unions. The council, which gained its present organizational form after the AFL-CIO merger in New York City in 1959, gives the union movement an inclusive interest group or peak association of substantial political influence, something the city's business organizations never have been able to develop.† But the Central Labor Council by no means speaks for all of organized labor in New York City. Several specialized joint councils exist independently—for example, the Ports Council for the maritime

---

*The most influential labor leader in the city is Harry Van Arsdale, Jr., head of the Central Trades and Labor Council, and of Local 3 of the International Brotherhood of Electrical Workers, the city's most important building trades union.

†Not until 1973 did a merger of the two most historically prominent business associations occur. The New York Chamber of Commerce and the New York City Commerce and Industry Association united to become the New York Chamber of Commerce and Industry.

unions, the Building and Construction Trades Council, and the 125,000-member Teamsters Union. Some important affiliates—for example, the Garment Workers' Unions and many public employee unions—have little in common with the Central Labor Council.

The union movement similarly is not immune to changes that have been occuring in the local economy. To some extent, the union movement has benefited from the growing service sector, but, on the whole, organized labor has not benefited from the tradeoff, now well advanced, between manufacturing jobs on one hand and white-collar and clerical jobs on the other. Most of the city's large private employers, its major corporations, are not heavily unionized; however, the city's declining manufacturing sector is heavily unionized. Had it not been for the rapid growth of city employee unions in the last decade, aggregate union membership in the city would have decreased.

The growth of public service unions is one facet of change that threatens to fragment the city's union movement and make it even more complex. The differences between public and private sector unions are substantial. Public employee unions in New York City deal with only a handful of employers, none of whom will be forced out of business by competition or move to another city. Public employee unions, particularly those made up of city government employees, on the whole have proved more vocal, more militant, and more successful in collective bargaining than private sector unions. In recent years, wages and benefits in the public sector have surpassed wages and benefits for most comparable unionized and nonunionized positions in the private sector.[13] This is a source of no small embarrassment and resentment among the city's older, more traditional union establishments.

One additional new element to which unions in New York City will have to adjust is the growing number of women and minority group members who are entering, and will continue to enter, the labor market.[14] The city's workforce is neither as male- nor as white-dominated as it once was. As formal and informal discriminatory barriers based on sex and race continue to fall, the nature of unionism will change, regardless of whether established unions resist or adapt to these changes. The record of the city's unions in this regard is spotty. Some unions have welcomed to their ranks new entrants to the city's labor force.* Other unions, particularly the skilled trades unions, have resisted pressures to incorporate new groups—pressures that emanate from minority groups, peer groups in the union movement, and government.

The problems facing the union movement in New York City, which are not all of recent origin, have helped in the development of what has been described as "mutual support" between labor and management.[15] The popular image of labor relations in New York City is one of intense conflict; in fact, however, to a surprising degree, cooperation and collaboration characterize union-management relations. In all likelihood this pattern will become even

---

*District Council 37, American Federation of State, County and Municipal Employees, and District 65, Retail, Wholesale, and Department Stores Union, have large and growing memberships based in large part on women, blacks, and Puerto Ricans.

more prevalent in the future, particularly with respect to union-management relations in industries facing intense competition.

The clearest example of union-management cooperation is the hiring hall. This practice, whereby unions virtually control hiring, has long been common practice in the maritime industry and remains substantially in effect in the building service, retail trade, hotel, and restaurant industries.[16] A second area of reciprocity concerns the relationship that is frequently evidenced between employer associations and unions, particularly where the association represents new or small businesses or businesses that are highly competitive. In such situations, union involvement in business management is freely sought by employers and may be substantial. In the electrical industry, a joint labor-management board exists for the purpose of protecting the industry generally and for resolving specific manpower and labor relations problems in particular.[17]

The same spirit pervades collective bargaining in several industries—the most prominent, perhaps, the apparel industry. Employment losses in apparel, which reached 64,000 jobs in the 1960s, have prompted unions, such as the International Ladies Garment Workers and the Amalgamated Clothing Workers, to exercise considerable restraint at the bargaining table with respect to wages and benefits and to enter into their own sales promotion efforts on behalf of the industry. In 1973 bindery and finishing employees in New York City even agreed to reduce scheduled pay increases by one-half in an attempt to improve the competitive position of their employers.[18]

In troubled industries the effect of labor-management relations on labor market information might be to improve the use and increase the utility of information for decision-making purposes. Nevertheless, the complex nature of the city's economy imposes awesome informational needs on business and union organizations. A fluid economic system in which there are approximately 1,000 separate labor unions and 225,000 employers (not to mention the roughly 4 million individuals in the labor force) poses obvious problems with respect to acquiring and disseminating relevant information about the economy for decisional purposes.

The complexity of economic life in New York City ensures that an adequate labor market information system will have to be extremely complex and inclusive. As is suggested in the next chapter, many of the perceived shortcomings in the existing stock of labor market information are directly related to the size and diversity of the city's economy.

THE CITY GOVERNMENT

The government of New York City incorporates within its structure and politics the diverse groups and interests found in the larger environment of the city. The interests of all but a few major groups in the city are represented somewhere in the giant apparatus of the city government. This does not mean that the interests of all groups are well served by decisions of the city government, but it does mean that decisions reached (as well as decisions that

118

are not reached) are subject generally to inputs of one kind or another by virtually all affected or potentially affected interest groups.

The essentially pluralist nature of the city government was described over a decade ago in what remains the definitive study of New York City politics.[19] During the last decade, the city government has grown even more pluralistic, with the result that decision making is increasingly incremental and, with respect to issues involving major change, increasingly difficult. New York City officials, particularly the mayor, have in recent years ceded or lost substantial political influence to other participants in the political process. Renewed efforts by the state government to dominate New York City affairs and the resurgence of local or community groups have caused decision-making authority to be redistributed upward and downward respectively, away from the city's major overhead actors—the mayor, budget and personnel officials, and legislators. The same phenomenon has occurred within the city government as a result of the growing influence of unionized civil servants.[20] These changes in the informal structure of power in the city government have been accompanied by formal changes in governmental responsibility that have weakened the influence of the city government in important functional areas, including transportation, education, and health services.*

The tendency toward reduced decision-making authority at the city government's central level has two important implications for this study. First, the linkages of the local government and economy, which are examined in the next section, are tenuous. The city government's efforts with respect to these linkages remain fragmented, reflecting the diverse interests of clientele and other groups rather than a coherent view of what the city government can or might do to improve the local economic and manpower systems. The capacity of the local government to integrate its activities with the local economy would appear to be severely constrained.

Second, the fact that authority within the city government is so fragmented raises certain questions regarding the ability of city officials to generate better labor market information and, more important, to make productive use of labor market information in their decisions affecting the local economy. Even if better information were available to policy makers, serious questions remain concerning the capacity of government officials to arrive at a consensus on the interpretation of data, to enact policies reflecting that consensus, and, finally, to implement policy decisions once they are reached. This second point is discussed in more detail in Chapter 7.

_____

*While the Board of Education has always maintained a high degree of autonomy from the mayor, this autonomy has increased since 1969, when the State school decentralization law changed the method of appointment to the Board from one of mayoral appointment to appointment by the five borough presidents. In 1968 a state agency, the Metropolitan Transportation Authority, took control of the New York City Transit Authority and Triborough Bridge and Tunnel Authority. In 1970 a semiautonomous Health and Hospitals Corporation replaced the city's Department of Health and Hospitals.

LINKAGES BETWEEN THE CITY
GOVERNMENT AND THE ECONOMY

The government of New York City is the single most important local participant in the city's economy; no other participant is as involved in the local economy in as many different and significant ways. The city government relates to the economy of New York City in five basic areas: employment, education, manpower training, economic development, and the delivery of services. Some of these linkages are far more direct than others, or at least are more easily observable. The employment linkage, for example, is easier to observe and evaluate than the service-delivery linkage. In all cases, however the constituencies involved are large in size, and the attendant policy and administrative problems complex in nature. In no instance can it be said that the information needs of decision or policy makers are readily definable, particularly in the two linkage areas that deal most directly with attempts to upgrade human resource potential—education and manpower training.

The city government's primary relationship with the local economy is best characterized as a condition in which the several linkages remain, for all practical purposes, separate. The strong tendency toward autonomous function stems in large part from the diversity of clientele groups or other groups affected by each function, as well as from the absence of influential political actors at the central level of city government who would be capable of playing a more integrative role. In Chapters 4 and 5 some of the constraints on educational adaptation to the changing economy, imposed by clientele and bureaucratic groups possessed of specialized and, in many cases, traditional educational interests, were indicated. Similar forces operate to prevent better adaptation among the several other activities of the city government that affect the local economy.

Employment

The city government is the city's largest employer. This nexus is the most direct linkage between the city government and the local economy. The City of New York employs approximately 400,000 persons, more than 11 percent of the total work force in the city. During the 1960s, when local government employment increased by 145,000, the city government was at the center of the city's employment growth.[2][1]

A large majority of the city government's employees are included in a civil service system that directly affects, among other things, the local government's hiring, promotion, and disciplinary procedures. This system is formally administered—in varying degrees—by the city's Department of Personnel, Civil Service Commission, Bureau of the Budget, and numerous line agencies. The State Civil Service Law and even the State Constitution sharply limit local discretion over the civil service system. Municipal employee unions also play an influential role in monitoring the civil service system. Whereas private employers might change hiring and promotion policies in response to labor market conditions, the city government's personnel system is highly resistant to pressures for change arising from either the external labor market or the internal public management process.[22]

The collective bargaining process in the city government involves a group of issues and actors quite different from those of the personnel process, but both processes evidence a similar degree of insulation from other facets of city government and from the local labor market. Negotiations for the city are conducted by the Office of Labor Relations, a mayoral agency. A separate office, the Office of Collective Bargaining, administers the city's collective bargaining program and also frequently plays the role of "third-party" in impasse situations. Budget personnel, line administrators, and legislative officials are involved only indirectly in the bargaining process. On balance, the dominant influence in the bargaining system is exerted by municipal employee unions.

Despite the important role that local government employment plays in the city's economy, city officials involved in municipal labor relations and collective bargaining seldom view their role in the larger context. Concerns, such as the maintenance of labor peace and, more recently, productivity, occupy their attention. For example, city officials involved in collective bargaining have not used the bargaining process, which allocates over half of the city government's more than $10 billion expense budget, to improve employment opportunities in the city. Hiring more employees in traditional service functions, some of which are severely understaffed, could only be accomplished within existing budgetary constraints through the adoption of a more cost-conscious policy at the bargaining table. Given the influence of municipal unions in collective bargaining, it is not difficult to understand why a policy of increasing employment through reductions in the size of bargaining settlements has not occurred.

On balance, the collective bargaining process has proved relatively immune to other intra- or extra-governmental pressures. The slowdown in economic activity in New York City beginning in 1969, and the resulting financial pressures within the city government, did not produce any appreciable change in the size of wage settlements. Indeed, in the uniformed services wages increased more rapidly after 1970 than before.[23] In several key services, including police, fire, sanitation, and education, departmental budgets were balanced by substantial reductions in the number of employees, achieved through an attrition policy.

Education

The city government's primary role as an intermediary in the local labor market is exercised through its enormous involvement in education at the pre-school, elementary, high school, college, and graduate levels. The city government operates or funds about 400 day-care centers; the Board of Education's almost 1,000 elementary and high schools service 1.1 million students, some 14 percent of the city's entire population; the City University of New York (CUNY) operates 18 separate institutions (including two-year community colleges, regular four-year colleges, and a graduate division) for approximately 240,000 students. While the city government by no means

121

monopolizes the delivery of education in New York City (for example, almost 400,000 of the city's elementary and high school students are enrolled in private schools), it carries the primary burden.

The Board of Education, with a budget in excess of $2 billion and more than 100,000 employees, is for all practical purposes a government within a government. The educational decision-making process, like the city's personnel and collective bargaining processes, is characterized by fragmentation and resistance to change. Control of the public school system lies outside of the mayor's authority. The seven-member Board of Education (two members are appointed by the mayor and one each by the five borough presidents), a school chancellor, and 32 local community school boards share control of the city's school system in a relationship as yet not clearly defined. A fourth powerful voice within the public school system is the United Federation of Teachers, a 70,000-member teachers' union that exerts its influence primarily through collective bargaining with the Board of Education, its representation on elected community school boards, and its power with respect to elected public officials.

In Chapters 4 and 5 some of the informational and decisional problems relating to curricular development in the city's vocational schools were presented. The Board of Education has faced substantial problems, on the whole, in changing the educational process. Since passage in 1969 of the school decentralization law, control of the educational process has been the major concern of the educational establishment—not the substance or quality of educational services. Linkages with other important facets of the city government remain poorly developed. Despite the fact that the city government, the city's largest employer, pays entry-level personnel as well as or better than the private sector, only one small program in the entire public school system is devoted to preparing high school students for direct entrance into the civil service.* Despite the open admissions program in higher education that permits virtually all high school graduates to enroll in a community college or regular four-year college, few linkages between the Boards of Education and of Higher Education have been developed to facilitate improved academic performance. The public school system has been slow, too, to integrate its educational efforts with demands for certain kinds of labor in the private sector. The city's business community continues to suffer from its inability to fill entry-level clerical jobs, a manpower shortage that, some believe, has contributed to the relocation of corporate activity away from New York City.[24]

Manpower Training

A third direct linkage between the local government and the economy is the sizeable manpower training effort in which the City of New York is

---

*The Franklin K. Lane High School operates a program designed to provide work-training and direct access to jobs in the City government. The director of the program has been forced to seek outside funding in an attempt to increase the limited scope of the program.

engaged. The primary purpose of such programs is to upgrade the supply of labor so that the skills of the resident labor force will better match the skills needed for jobs that are or will be available in the city. The mismatch between occupational structure and manpower supply is pronounced in New York City, but probably no more so than in many large urban labor markets. Ginzberg points out that even with the relatively high educational requirements associated with white-collar jobs in New York City, a high school diploma suffices for about three out of every four jobs in the city (p. 78).[25] On balance, the upgrading process in New York City has been considerable. But despite the fact that the city government spends more than $150 million annually on manpower training, it is widely acknowledged that the training programs are not adequate in terms of scope or performance.

Fragmentation of government involvement in this area is more pronounced than in any of the other four linkage areas. From an organizational viewpoint the city's manpower training program has been chaotic. Recognition of this fact led to the creation of the New York City Manpower Area Planning Council, which is designed to play a coordinating and integrating role.*

The city's major manpower agency is the Manpower and Career Development Agency located within the Human Resources Administration, but several other city government agencies are either directly or indirectly involved in manpower programs,† In addition, the New York State Employment Service, the federal government (through four separate departments or agencies), labor unions, and private businesses also participate in the local manpower training process. If those who finance and oversee New York City's manpower programs are a disparate group, so too are its managers. The influence of business, labor, and, particularly, community groups in the management and control of manpower training programs is substantial.

It is difficult to evaluate the city's manpower training efforts from the outside, in part because until recently little evaluation has occurred on the inside. The *Comprehensive Manpower Plan for New York City, Fiscal Year 1974* includes fairly detailed program assessments of some of the major manpower programs in New York City. Volume I of the *Plan* outlines the newly-devised rating system for program performance, and Volume II presents a wealth of data for selected programs having to do with the demographic outline of clients, training procedures, placement and retention, and costs.[26] The performance rating system, unrefined as it is, provides some worthwhile data and conclusions that should permit manpower policy makers to approach the funding and administration of separate programs on a more rational basis than in the past.

---

*The second annual report of the Manpower Area Planning Council, *Comprehensive Manpower Plan for New York City, Fiscal Year 1974*, indicates that the council has made substantial planning and informational gains in the past year.

†Other city government agencies include the Board of Education, the Board of Higher Education, the Community Development Agency, the Addiction Services Agency, the Department of Correction, Model Cities, Health Services Administration, and the Youth Services Agency.

Both the 1973 and 1974 comprehensive manpower plans underscore the importance of job creation in New York City and the difficulties involved in upgrading skill levels through institutional manpower programs. The major manpower policy adopted for fiscal 1974 is that "money for manpower programs should be expended only where there are firm job commitments or an absolute assurance that a market for these jobs exists."[27] In addition, on-the-job training programs, as opposed to institutional training programs, will receive funding priority.

With respect to information problems, the city government's manpower officials have made considerable progress in the past year in developing an internal information system based on program evaluation data for use in their planning and funding decisions. However, a lack of external labor market information still exists with respect to locating job opportunities in individual businesses and industrial sectors. The success of the New York City Manpower Area Planning Council in upgrading its internal information base provides some hope that the necessary information about employment opportunities in the local job market will be acquired, but the lack of an adequate understanding of local job opportunities remains a substantial informational problem.

Economic Development

While more than $150 million is spent annually on manpower training programs in New York City, in fiscal year 1973 the city government appropriated only $34 million to its Economic Development Administration (EDA), the agency charged with providing direction and policy guidance for the economic development of the city. And of that sum, $25 million was spent to service debt on items in the city government's capital budget and for fringe benefits to EDA employees. The Commercial and Industrial Development program within EDA, which is specifically designed to "encourage and stimulate general business developments within the City," employed 95 persons and received $1.7 million in fiscal 1973, less on both counts than in the previous year.[28] Since the city lost 54,000 jobs in 1970, 130,000 jobs in 1971, and 73, 000 jobs in 1972, the city government's commitment to developing this fourth linkage with the local economy—that is, to help stimulate business activity—seems suspect, particularly in light of the widespread consensus concerning the importance of job expansion in the city.

The Economic Development Administration is not the only agency of the city government directly concerned with economic development. The City Planning Commission, which is charged with the responsibility of guiding the future growth and development of the city, and which shapes that growth directly through its formulation of the draft capital budget and zoning policies, is also an important participant. But the influence of the City Planning Commission on the developmental process has never fulfilled the expectations surrounding the commission's creation in 1938. The short-lived (though long-awaited) master plan for New York City, which was produced in 1969 and tabled in 1973, is illustrative of the limited ability of the City Planning Commission to formulate and oversee the implementation of coherent land-use policies for developmental purposes. The growing influence of the 62 community (planning) boards in the city suggests that future planning efforts of the commission will be less oriented towards economic development than in the past, given the tendency of local or community groups to forego concern for economic or institutional expansion in favor of local "amenity" improvements, such as parks, playgrounds, housing, and so on.

Comprehensive planning for industrial and economic development purposes is frustrated, too, by the influence of the Board of Estimate in capital budget and zoning determination. The political balance of power within the Board of Estimate remains such that the respective borough presidents can generally block systematic development and zoning plans of which they disapprove. The orientation of the Board of Estimate and, increasingly, of the City Planning Commission is local, not citywide.

One final element that merits emplicit recognition is the emerging influence of locally-based community groups in the city's political process. In many respects, community groups, whether ad hoc or formal, have become an important labor market intermediary in New York City. As mentioned above, community groups are deeply involved in the administration of manpower programs, but the most pervasive influence of community groups on the local labor market is registered through their impact on developmental decisions, particularly where institutional or facilities expansion is involved. Only rarely do community groups play an affirming role when issues are raised about the relocation or expansion of facilities, not only industrial plants, office buildings, and roads, but sometimes even schools and hospitals. The bias of community groups is, generally speaking, toward the preservation of existing neighborhood patterns; the expansion of local job opportunities ordinarily ranks as a low priority.

Very few major developmental decisions are reached any longer in New York City without substantial input from local groups. Sometimes that input causes developmental decisions reached by others—principally, businesses and the city government—to be unmade, as in the decision finally taken in 1970 by Alexander's not to construct a branch department store on the upper West Side of Manhattan. More often the effect of local involvement is to cause decisions reached earlier and elsewhere to be modified, as in the case of the containerport controversy in South Brooklyn in 1973. Increasingly, the expansion of commercial facilities in New York City is being carried out over water, air, or in unused land space because of the influence of local groups in the developmental decision-making process.

Delivery of Basic Services

A more diffuse but still very important linkage between the local government and economy concerns all the many service functions performed by the government, other than those in the areas of employment, education, manpower training, and economic development. The local government's activities in housing, transportation, health, the criminal justice system, environmental protection, and welfare, to mention only a few examples, affect the functioning of the labor market in myriad ways, the effectiveness of the labor market in turn affects the capacity of the city government to provide basic services. The impact of government services on the quality of life in New York City, and the impact of this variable on the city's economy, is impossible to measure but seemingly easy to underestimate. A single instance of official laxity or inefficiency—for example, a failure to arrest, indict, or convict a major heroin dealer—might undo the cumulative efforts of dozens of people and an investment of hundreds of thousands of dollars to educate and train a handful of young people.

It is in this general area that one is able to see most clearly the effect of governmental fragmentation on governmental planning and performance. Not only is the delivery of a single service often frustrated by fragmentation of power and responsibility, but positive linkages between different services remain poorly developed. Diffusion of responsibility for developing a rational transportation system in and around New York City has not only produced an irrational transportation system but helped to promote a situation in which other developmental decisions have been reached without serious consideration for their effect on transportation. The 1973 decision to construct a new convention center in Manhattan along the Hudson River between 44th and 45th Streets is a case in point. Since the nearest subway station is close to a mile from the site selected for the convention center, nearly all visitors, including freight deliverers, will have to travel to the center by truck, car, taxi, or bus. Traffic in the area—which includes the outmoded West Side Highway, entrance routes to the Lincoln Tunnel, and a new passenger ship terminal—is already extremely congested, but little attention was paid to congestion and air pollution problems in the decision-making process leading to the planned convention center.

The systemic nature of urban processes—that is, the way in which one problem feeds on another or one policy response touches off a series of secondary and often unanticipated consequences—is now widely recognized, though the precise primary and secondary relationships are not yet well understood.[29] The complexity of the system often leads to decision making that exacerbates rather than ameliorates problems, particularly where decisions are reached in the absence of adequate information about either problem causation or policy consequence. Examples of this phenomenon are numerous, running from the macro to the micro level. Perhaps the single most important historical example concerns the impact of the Federal Housing Administration and its successor agencies on metropolitan growth; by subsidizing home building instead of rehabilitation, the federal government in effect subsidized the flight of the while middle-class from the central city to suburbs, where vacant land for new housing was available. The same consequence, of course, was (and still is) served by the nation's urban transportation policies, which have made it relatively easy and inexpensive to commute on freeways from suburban homes to central city jobs.

However, substantial advances in data and theory, which may reduce the proability of "error" in urban policy formulation, do not spare the policy-formulating process from the dictates of the political process. The Lower Manhattan Expressway project is a classic example of the complex decision-making environment in which city government officials operate. For over a decade the project has been alternately scheduled and cancelled, the timing of its periodic rise and fall always corresponding closely to the proximity of a mayoral election. Deciding whether this project, or dozens like it, is rational or desirable from the overall perspective of the city's development is, at best, difficult. Proponents as well as opponents of new departures are usually well armed with data that "conclusively demonstrate" the nexus between their respective positions and the "public interest." In such an environment the most important information public officials use in decision making might have very little to do with "labor market" information.

NOTES

1. Boris Yavitz and Dean W. Morse, *The Labor Market: An Information System* (New York: Praeger, 1973), p. 35.

2. Ibid., pp. 35-36.

3. Boris Yavitz and Dean W. Morse, "Labor Market Information," in *New York Is Very Much Alive* Eli Ginzberg et al., eds. (New York: McGraw-Hill, 1973), p. 216.

4. For a lucid exposition of the forces affecting the character of urban economic growth, see Wilbur Thompson, *A Preface to Urban Economics* (Baltimore: The Johns Hopkins Press, 1965), pp. 15-60. Thompson suggests that a "rachet-like" principle works when urban economies reach a certain size that "locks in" diversity of function and ensures future economic growth.

5. U.S. Department of Labor, Bureau of Labor Statistics, Middle Atlantic Regional Office, *1972 Year-End Report of Employment, Prices and Earnings in New York City* (Washington, D.C.: Government Printing Office, December 1972), p. 6.

6. In 1967 the average number of employees by type of business was as follows: manufacturing, 31; wholesale trade, 12; retail trade and services, 6. These averages were computed from data in New York State Department of Commerce, *New York State Business Fact Book,* (1972), Part I.

7. U.S. Department of Labor, Bureau of Labor Statistics, Middle Atlantic Regional Office, op. cit., p. 6.

8. Ginzberg et al., eds., op. cit., p. 83.

9. Robert Lichtenberg, *One-Tenth of a Nation* (Cambridge, Mass.: Harvard University Press, 1960), p. 32.

10. State Study Commission for New York City, *New York City: Economic Base and Fiscal Capacity* (April 1973), pp. 1-24.

11. See Alice Cook and Lois Gray, "Labor Relations in New York City," *Industrial Relations* 5 (May 1966): 92-93.

12. See Yavitz and Morse, *The Labor Market. . . ,* pp. 63-72.

13. U.S. Department of Labor, Bureau of Labor Statistics, Middle Atlantic Regional Office, *Wages and Benefits of Municipal Government Workers in New York City* (Washington, D.C.: Government Printing Office, June 1971).

14. Job openings arising from economic growth and turnover are and will be concentrated in occupations that are largely filled by women, according to

estimates of the New York State Department of Labor. It has also been estimated that close to one-half of the future entrants to the city's job market will be black or Hispanic. See Ginzberg et al., eds., op. cit., p. 109.

15. Cook and Gray, op. cit., pp. 95-96.

16. Ibid., p. 91.

17. Ibid., p. 95.

18. "Bookbinders Unite to Defer a Pay Raise," *New York Times*, May 20, 1973, p. 38.

19. Wallace Sayre and Herbert Kaufman, *Governing New York City*, (New York: Norton, 1965).

20. Raymond Horton, *Municipal Labor Relations in New York City*, (New York: Praeger, 1973).

21. U.S. Department of Labor, Bureau of Labor Statistics, Middle Atlantic Regional Office, *Some Facts Relating to the New York City Scene* (Washington, D.C.: Government Printing Office, April 1970), p. 5.

22. For an interesting analysis of the local government's civil service system, see E. S. Savas and Sigmund Ginsburg, "The Civil Service: A Meritless System," *The Public Interest*, 32 (Summer 1973): 70-85.

23. Indeed, in the uniformed services, wages increased more rapidly after 1970 than before. Horton, op. cit., pp. 95-96.

24. Economic Development Council, *New York City's Clerical Manpower Requirements and Problems* (New York: The Council, 1970), pp. 17-22.

25. Ginzberg et al., op. cit., p. 78. A generally optimistic picture of New York City's position in this regard is painted in *New York Is Very Much Alive.*

26. Manpower Area Planning Council, *Comprehensive Manpower Plan for New York City, Fiscal Year 1974.* See particularly Vol. I, pp. 41-50, for the council's rating system.

27. Ibid., Vol. I, p. 1.

28. *Expense Budget of the City of New York, 1972-73*, p. 76.

29. A number of scholarly works in the urban area have explicitly treated the systemic nature of urban problems and policy. Among the most important of these works are Wilbur Thompson, *A Preface to Urban Economics* (Baltimore: The Johns Hopkins Press, 1965); Edward Banfield, *The Unheavenly City* (Boston: Little Brown, 1968); Jay Forrester, *Urban Dynamics* (Cambridge, Mass.: MIT Press, 1969).

The search for improved labor market information is based on the straightforward premise that better information will produce more rational decisions that, in turn, should produce a more efficient labor market. Efforts to operationalize this concept at the level of direct labor market participants—for example, specific job seekers and offerers—have been considerable and are manifested in a wide variety of formal private and governmental activities, ranging from want ads to job banks.

However, as is indicated in this chapter, effecting an improved information system with respect to indirect participants—that is, institutions whose decisions shape the flows and arrivals of direct participants to the specific employer-employee exchange—is an exceedingly complicated task. For one thing, the large number of intermediaries and the broad scope of their decision-making concerns ensure that information in its totality, in order to be relevant to individual actors, must be far-ranging in detail and substance. A direct labor market participant—a corporation seeking to expands its clerical staff, perhaps—might find that information limited to prevailing clerical wages is sufficient for its decision-making needs; however, the same institution functioning as an indirect labor market participant—for example, a corporation considering a decision to relocate its headquarters in the New York suburban area—would require a much broader information base. In addition to data on comparative suburban wage rates, comparative information concerning, among others, tax rates, transportation lines, demographic and labor force characteristics, housing supplies, and recreational facilities might be sought by a corporation contemplating a relocation decision.

A second factor that complicates the information-institution linkage when indirect labor market participants are being considered is conflict among information users. When a prospective employer and a prospective employee—the classic direct labor market participants—circulate or seek information about each other, both parties assumedly desire an exchange or decision that will be mutually beneficial. However, in many instances indirect participants seek information in the hope that it can be used to help produce decisions not in the interest of other participants. Some decisions for which information is needed or used are of approximate zero-sum decisions. In such situations information can be seen most clearly as a resource of power. Data are susceptible to manipulation (for example, hoarding until a propitious moment for release) and criticism (often justified) for being false or misleading. Not surprisingly, many such instances occur in the public arena where decisions or prospective decisions often involve relatively clear-cut "winners" and "losers."

The controversy in New York over reform of public employee pensions illustrates well the complex role information can play in a decision-making setting charged with political interests and conflict. Each of the three major intermediaries examined in this study, but particularly the business community and public employee unions, approached resolution of the issue from separate, essentially antagonistic positions. Clearly, several detailed studies of the city government's pension system originally provided some of the impetus for pension reform; however, these studies, along with studies provided for rebuttal purposes by prounion forces, played a minor role in the actual resolution of the issue, largely because the politics of the issue politicized the data—in essence, rendered them neutral. When the pension system was eventually changed, the vote in both houses of the state legislature was strictly on party lines, with Republicans, led by the governor, favoring reform, and Democrats opposing reform.[1] Information played a role in the outcome because it spurred initial interest in pension reform, but on balance certainly not an important clarifying role for legislators with respect to their decision-making options.

A third major hindrance to the development of a system whereby indirect labor market participants can be equipped with better information is the poorly developed state of theory to explain the ways that urban economies and labor markets function and, equally important, effective policy responses to economic malfunctions. In order to develop or acquire better labor market information, both those who produce and those who use labor market information must better understand the kind of information that is relevant for their purposes, whether the purposes be description, prediction, or policy remediation.

The benefits from having improved labor market information, better decisions, and a more efficient labor force could be great—not only for New York City itself but for the region and the nation as well. However, the size and diversity of the city seriously complicate the way to realizing the desired linkage between information and its users.

THE EXISTING STOCK OF LABOR
MARKET INFORMATION

The amount of available information about New York City's economy is staggering, yet those persons who are engaged in research or who use information in their various decision-making capacities almost universally label the existing stock of information inadequate. This seeming paradox arises from the overwhelming diversity of those who produce and those who use labor market information in the city. Several common characterizations of the city's labor market information are discussed immediately below. What is clear is how closely these informational shortcomings are related to the nature of the local economy and to the interactions of its major participants.

Information Gaps

One commonly perceived shortcoming of the city's labor market information is its lack of completeness. The size and dynamic nature of the city's economy virtually ensure the existence of substantial informational lacunae. In fact, very little is known about some clearly important facets of the city's economy. For example, despite the huge commitment, both public and private, to manpower training programs, very little is known about their effectiveness.* The nexus between the local economy and governmental policies of expenditure and employment, particlarly with respect to the city government, is an important but virtually untouched area of analysis.

Commutation patterns into, out of, and within the city, which should affect decision making in regard to transportation and housing, among other things, in New York City remain a mystery, except at the level of gross commutation flows, which offer policy makers little guidance. Reverse commutation, the flow of city residents to suburban jobs, is substantially greater than was commonly thought for many years. Because mass transit links between the city and its suburbs come together in central Manhattan, real or potential reverse commuters who live in Brooklyn, Queens, or the Bronx face difficulty using existing mass transit facilities to travel to and from work. Because many potential reverse commuters are from low-income families and do not own cars, one method of improving their access to suburban jobs would be for the city government to provide bus service to reverse commuters. Lacking an appreciable understanding of where reverse commuters live and work, remediation of their transportation problems by providing direct bus service is difficult.

While nearly everyone interviewed in connection with this study commented that the quantity and quality of information in the city was increasing, a substantial number of important areas remain the subject of little data-oriented analysis. This phenomenon, it must be added, is due in no small part to the unwillingness of key labor market intermediaries themselves to become the subject of investigation. The city government, in particular, often is an unwilling subject of investigation and frequently an unwilling purveyor of

---

*The dramatically upgraded quality of evaluation of New York City manpower programs, as evidenced in the second report of the New York City Manpower Area Planning Council, *Comprehensive Manpower Plan for New York City, Fiscal Year 1974* , suggests that if the Council continues its present orientation, this particular information gap will be substantially closed.

information. By 1972, for example, an ethnic survey of city government employees, begun in 1962 by the city's Commission on Human Rights, with the full support of the mayor, was stalled because several key city government agencies and municipal employee unions refused to cooperate, fearing that publication of the data might lead to increased pressures for a quota system in hiring.

Dated Information

A scholar's bane as well as decision maker's burden is the fact that much of the information concerning the city's economy is not timely. Dated information presents less of a problem for policy makers or planners who are concerned with fundamental policy issues, such as restructuring the government's tax base to make it more responsive to local economic growth.[2] But the lack of timely information seriously interferes with some public efforts. As was mentioned in Chapter 6, manpower officials of the city government need not only accurate estimates of long-range manpower demands for planning purposes but also current data on job openings, if they are to be successful in changing the short-run orientation of existing manpower programs.

The tendency in New York City is for major studies of the city's economy not to be followed by related and on-going research efforts. The case of the New York Metropolitan Region Study will serve as an example. This study, which was directed by Raymond Vernon, produced a number of books in the late 1950s and 1960s discussing the city's and the region's economies. On balance, they painted a glowing picture of the city's economic future. But the failure to follow up with continuing research may have prevented policy makers from reacting to danger signs that appeared in the mid-1960s.

It is not at all atypical in the research outputs of any given year to find data that are more than a few years old. This is not so much a reflection of the data-gathering techniques of any individual or group as it is a consequence of the dynamics of the information system in general. Only a few groups, such as the Middle Atlantic Regional Office of the U.S. Bureau of Labor Statistics, with specific mandates and interests, are heavily involved in current and periodic analysis. And often the data provided by such groups are of a general nature, with limited utility for groups with specialized information needs.

Poor Quality

The charge is frequently made by users (more than by producers) of labor market information that data are unreliable. The charge might be correct in some instances, but the alleged unreliability of information often reflects the inconsistent manner in which data are presented from study to study and the fact that many information producers generate information with little or no concern for the ways their data will eventually be used or for the people who will use the data. To repeat a point made earlier, criticism having to do with the accuracy of data often rests on political rather than empirical foundations.

The nonstandardized manner in which data are presented by suppliers of labor market information does represent a problem for information users. The functional mesh between the interests of those who supply and those who demand labor market information in New York City is incomplete. For example, the Middle Atlantic Regional Office of the U.S. Bureau of Labor Statistics, for obvious reasons having to do with its role in the federal bureaucracy, provides considerable comparative labor market data that have relatively little utility for many local information users. Further, regional BLS data are frequently exhibited in official publications in the form of bar charts and graphs that indicate trends and percentage increases or decreases without providing base data.[3] New York State agencies, particularly the Departments of Labor and Commerce, typically present economic data concerning New York City in highly detailed tabular form, leaving extrapolation almost entirely up to users.[4] The various presentational forms have their own heuristic and empirical strengths and weaknesses, but from the perspective of information users the variety of expositional forms is often frustrating.

Contradictory Data

Those who deal with information about New York City constantly are faced with the problem of reconciling or choosing between contradictory or inconsistent data. Again, the problem of contradictory data arises in large part from the multitude of primary data sources and, in many cases, from discrepancies among classifications. As a classic example, a 1971 study of employment patterns in New York City, conducted by a reputable research organization, its data obtained from a computer tape furnished by the Social Security Administration, indicated, among other things, that manufacturing employment increased during the mid-1960s and that employment in wholesale and retail trade decreased sharply.[5] While some valuable information about the employment prospects of racial minorities was discovered as a result of the study, the data on sectoral employment were grossly inconsistent with other research findings because of conflicting classification techniques.

A similar problem pervades analysis of the city's racial and ethnic groups, particularly with respect to ascertaining the size of the city's nonwhite, nonblack population. Estimates of the city's Puerto Rican (or Hispanic or Spanish-speaking) population vary strikingly, at least in part because various analysts use different ethnic classification techniques.

Dissemination of Data

Perhaps the most frequently expressed criticism of the city's labor market information system has to do not with the content of existing data but with its limited dissemination among potential users. No on-going or organized procedure for the distribution of labor market information exists in New York City. Informal communication and distribution links have been built up, and extensive mailing lists exist in the offices of some information producers, but adequate transmission of labor market information remains a serious problem.

Furthermore, given some of the reasons for the limited, inefficient system of information dissemination that now exists, improving distribution will not be easy. Because information is a power resource, no intermediary with important stakes in the local economy will freely choose to distribute information it possesses if that information is potentially damaging to its interests. This is true for government no less than for the other major labor market participants.

A related point is that information is sometimes disseminated in order to advance an actor's interests even when the information is inaccurate or misleading. In response to criticism of high municipal employee salaries in New York City, city government officials in 1973 released to the press a study purporting to show that between 1966 and 1971 labor costs for city government employees rose more slowly than in most other large cities.[6] Careful analysis of the study, and the background data from which the study was prepared, indicate that the study was (at best) misleading.

In addition to being a resource of power, information is costly to acquire. Many specialized producers and users of high quality information—for example, a corporation which has retained a consulting firm to provide information and advice on a decision of some consequence—have no incentives whatever to distribute the information produced in such a relationship. In such a situation, the competitive reality of the marketplace works much like the conflictual reality of politics with respect to the dissemination of information. Neither the corporate user of information nor the corporate producer of such information gains from external dissemination of information produced and acquired in such a relationship.

To summarize, the real and perceived problems with the existing stock of labor market information in New York City are in large part, though not completely, explained by the nature of the local economy. The system of accumulation, distribution, and usage of labor market information, like the labor market itself, is decentralized and fragmented. No producers of information combine the requisite resources or incentives to approach labor market information in a systematic, inclusive manner. Similarly, no users of information, at least among the nongovernmental users, require or demand a comprehensive labor market information system. Generally speaking, the linkage between production and use of labor market information is poorly defined in New York City.

Despite the overall weakness of that linkage, there are important areas in which it exists; and where production and use are integrated, information appears to be, on balance, at least adequate for decision-making purposes. The fact that some information needs *are* being met suggests that something more than the decentralized, fragmented structure of users and producers and the competitive nature of many decisions for which information is used might be weighing against the development of a better information system.

In those instances in which the production of labor market information and its use are best integrated, the users of information have a clear understanding of the kind of information they need. This understanding, whether the product of experience or theory, enables many users of information to develop that information internally or to purchase it externally from a specialized consulting firm or a trade association.[7] For example, in the area of wage determination—clearly an important element in the definition of the local labor market—little evidence suggests that most major employing institutions or unions in New York City suffer from inadequate information. Because employers and unions are regularly (and have long been) involved in salary-setting processes, they possess a clear understanding of the kinds of data that are necessary for decision-making purposes. And employees and unions possess a variety of means of generating that information: internally through trade or union associations of which they are members, and externally from specialized consulting firms.

Put simply, the absence of accepted theory concerning the functioning of urban labor markets is a substantial impediment to the development of better labor market information. Intermediaries with considerable experience in performing certain functions related to the labor market, such as wage determination, know from experience—if not from a theoretical appreciation of how urban labor markets function—what information they need.

However, as we have seen, the linkages of each major intermediary to the labor market are several. When the linkages are relatively new—for example, as in the efforts of business, unions, and the city government to provide specialized manpower training services to prospective employees—the absence of experience or of theory restricts the supply of labor market information. Knowing little about the causes of a given problem and not understanding the types of corrective decisions that can or should be made leads to a situation in which users of information do not know what information they need, and producers of information do not know what information to supply.

Forrester, a leading critic of conventional empirical techniques and policy analysis in the urban setting, emphasizes the importance of theory for the acquisition and use of information:

> In the social sciences failure to understand systems is often blamed on inadequate data. The barrier to progress in social systems is not lack of data. We have vastly more information than we use in an orderly and organized way. The barrier is deficiency in the existing theories of structure.[8]

This problem is particularly pronounced with respect to policy making in the city government. The "science" of urban policy making has not yet reached even rudimentary theoretical levels. Lacking a more developed theoretical understanding of the ways that urban systems function, particularly with respect to the policy interface between urban governments and urban economies, information will continue to be inadequate in some of the same ways the existing stock of labor market information is inadequate.[9] If there are gaps in the city's information base, and if the approach to information-gathering and

135

the presentation of information are not systematic, it is partly because information producers and users do not have a complete grasp of the sort of information that is relevant.

TOWARD AN IMPROVED LABOR MARKET INFORMATION SYSTEM

Understanding how the structure of New York City's economy and politics affects the existing supply of labor market information is important because a better information base will have to be constructed within essentially the same framework. The large number of employing institutions and labor unions is not likely to decrease rapidly in the future; the city's economic functions probably will become more diversified, not less; the city government is, if anything, likely to grow more fragmented politically. Even if centralizing the production of labor market data were to prove possible (this approach is discussed shortly), the users of that data—and thus the data itself—would remain a large, heterogeneous lot.

It seems extremely doubtful that any new institutional format can be devised in either the private or the public sector that could successfully orchestrate a close relationship between the production and use of labor market information in New York City. A system that relied on the marketplace to generate information might produce high quality information specifically tied to user needs, but the specialized needs of individual users would militate against the likelihood that a systematic, wide-ranging data base would ever emerge. And, as previously noted, the private market for this production service would be destroyed if the information supplied to specific consumers was ever made widely available.

Neither does it seem likely that any centralized governmental agency could ever assume a systematic information-gathering function that could produce data sufficiently varied and specific to meet the needs of private and public users. Creating an information "superagency" with this broad mission in the government of New York City would be an enormously costly and highly uncertain venture. In addition, there is little assurance that the quality of information produced by a public agency would match the quality of information produced under the existing, albeit decentralized, system.

This suggests that a more realistic approach to upgrading the city's information base might be found along a more incremental path—at least for the present. One such proposal to improve the city's labor market information system calls for the creation of a consortium of major information users in New York City. According to Yavitz and Morse who are the proponents of the consortium approach, the principle problem with the city's data base is "the lack of coordination, analysis, and adequate dissemination of the immense body of information which now is in existence."[10] An information consortium would be charged with integrating "to the maximum extent possible both private and public sources of information relevant to the city's labor markets."[11] A consortium like the one proposed by Yavitz and Morse probably would improve the distribution of existing labor market information and in so doing increase the net amount of information available. Yavitz and Morse are correct no doubt in suggesting that data needed by one labor market participant "may lie in the files of another participant."[12]

It would seem important that the government of New York City play a leading role in such a consortium. Because of the city government's many links with the local economy, the city government is itself potentially a rich data source. Equally important, the local government needs better information for its many decision-making responsibilities. Some specific proposals for improving the city's labor market data base, built around the consortium approach, are discussed in Chapter 8.

Even if the means for improving the labor market information system in New York City do exist, an important question remains to be examined: How much positive impact would better information have on the functioning of the local labor market?

THE POTENTIAL OF IMPROVED LABOR MARKET INFORMATION

If there were a labor market information system in New York City that provided more information of a higher quality to the major intermediaries examined, marginal improvements in the overall functioning of the local economy probably would result. Information can only be valuable if those who are provided with information are able to use it in a consequential manner: this is true for direct participants as well as indirect participants. Because of a variety of endogenous and exogenous variables, an individual jobseeker, no matter how much labor market information he possesses, can be unable to use the information to effect successful entry into the job market. He can be psychologically or physically unequipped to work, or he can be barred from work by the imposition of some external barrier—perhaps an age requirement or the absence of means for commuting to work.

The ability of indirect participants to effectively use labor market information is complicated by a variety of constraints involving information use. This seems to be the case, particularly with respect to governments—at least some governments. Within government, better information might not produce an official consensus on policy; official consensus on a policy might not produce a decision; a decision reached might not be implemented; even if all those conditions are met, exogenous factors over which governments have little effective control might render a decision inconsequential.

The above suggests that the internal structures of power and authority possessed by various labor market intermediaries are important determinants of the potential efficacy of labor market information. If the existing stock of labor market information is largely dependent on structural characteristics of the local economy, the potential that improved labor market information holds seems largely dependent on structural characteristics of information users. In addition, this line of reasoning suggests that some intermediaries more than others—and some economies more than others—will benefit from improved labor market information. (This point will be discussed in the concluding section of this chapter.)

That the ability of an intermediary to benefit from improved labor market information is dependent upon its ability to use that information can be seen clearly by examining the government of New York City. In Chapter 6 we examined the five primary processes that link the local government to the local economy: employment, education, manpower training, economic development, and service delivery. Given existing patterns of structure, conflict, and power (endogenous variables), better information is not likely to substantially improve any of these linkages. And even if the nexus between information and decision making were established, exogenous variables over which the city government has no effective control might severely limit the effectiveness of local governmental decisions. Federal fiscal policy or national economic trends can negate the effect of even the most salutary local initiatives.

The employment linkage is most affected by the city government's relationship with municipal employee unions. It was noted in Chapter 6 that the dynamics of the city government's municipal labor relations process forced the major participants in that process to be primarily concerned with traditional labor-management concerns, such as, salaries, fringe and pension benefits, and personnel administration, and deflected the attention of participants from viewing the labor relations process in a broader way related to expanding employment opportunities in New York City.

Translating information into decisions that would improve the employment linkage—for example, increasing the number of city government employees within existing budgetary constraints—would be very difficult. Even if the potential for such a policy change were demonstrated conclusively in an informational sense, it is unlikely that the various city government officials involved in the labor relations process would immediately arrive at a consensus on the desirability of pursuing the policy. Budget officials interested in increased productivity and manpower officials interested in expanding job opportunities might view increasing public employment via this mechanism as desirable; political advisors to the mayor and negotiators, who must be mindful of the attitudes of civil service union leaders, would probably not be favorably disposed. And even if a consensus were reached among city government officials on the desirability of explicitly linking collective bargaining with expanded employment opportunities, no "decision" of consequence would be reached until collective bargaining agreements embodying the principle were signed with municipal unions. Due to the existing balance of power in the municipal labor relations process it is difficult to imagine such a decision ever being reached.

This situation, though only hypothetical, highlights some of the internal characteristics that often render the informational component in the city government something less than important. Diversity of opinion within the government is pronounced, reflecting the larger pluralism of New York City. Reaching consensus on a given policy involves a heavy weighing of political considerations that might have little to do with the substance or teachings of labor market information. Formalizing a policy decision in the city government is usually accomplished by bargaining, only rarely by fiat. Finally, the power relationships involving city government officials and those groups with which they must bargain are often such that the policy goals of city government officials are not realized.

A similar conclusion is also suggested concerning the potential of information for improving other decision-making arenas linking the government's activities and the local economy. Since very little information about the city government's manpower programs has been generated, it is difficult to consider the ways that better information might affect decision making. The fragmented, uncoordinated approach to manpower administration in New York City gives little reason for optimistically believing that improved information can play an important role, at least at present.

No amount of information upgrading is likely to convince the various groups competing for control of the city's public school system that controlling the school system is a less important concern than finding ways for improving the system. Until the question of control of the school system is resolved, questions concerning the quality of education will probably remain unresolved. Of course, none of the participants engaged in the educational power struggle is willing to concede that questions of educational control and educational performance can be separated. (Whether or not it is the case that they can be separated is irrelevant for the purpose of inquiry at hand.) Until some stable decision-making structure emerges, information probably will not play a prominent role in the formulation of educational policy.

In the areas of education and manpower training one important element that affects the capacity of city government officials to utilize information is the heavy involvement of local or community-oriented groups in policy making and administration. Community groups are also increasingly influential in the area of economic development, particularly where the issue at hand concerns the location of tangible facilities, such as office buildings, factories, hospitals, and roads.* Community groups—whether formal groups, such as the 62 community boards of the City government, or ad hoc groups that emerge in response to single issues—represent generally conservative forces in the city's economic development process. Their commitment to preserving neighborhoods is intense, and they possess a variety of political tactics that they can employ to resist private as well as governmental decisions. No amount of information is likely to dissuade community opposition to certain projects designed specifically or generally to stimulate the city's economy. The traditional role of the City Planning Commission, a key governmental participant in the planning process, has changed substantially in recent years as the input of community groups within the commission and before the Board of Estimate has increased. The present chairman of the City Planning Commission, unlike his predecessors, is attempting to explicitly restructure the planning process to

---

*Community groups, in addition to affecting the local economy through their impact on economic development decisions and heavy involvement in running manpower training programs, also employ a substantial number of people. The city government's poverty program, for example, provides jobs in community organizations to approximately 15,000 persons.

provide direct and formal access for local community planning boards. Some persons argue, possibly with some validity, that this will eventually work to make local groups more responsive to informational inputs and less responsive to "emotive" inputs from community groups. Bureaucratic co-opting, which seems to be at work presently in the planning process in other areas of the city's politics, such as in the poverty program, has served this end to some extent.

Again, the desirability or undesirability of the community movement is not the issue here. The question is, what effect does the community movement have on the potential of the city government to utilize labor market information in strengthening its links with the local economy? To the extent that the government increasingly incorporates specific groups into its decision-making processes, its potential is probably diminished.

The point was made earlier, and it will be amplified in Chapter 8, that although the government of New York City possibly could play an important role in contributing to the production of improved labor market information in the city, the fragmented nature of the city government makes the likelihood of the government's being a major beneficiary in terms of using improved information slim. Not all purposive institutions are equipped alike to utilize information for decision-making purposes. The government of New York City, from the perspective of information utilization, clearly suffers from its complex, highly conflictive internal power structure. Some of the internal political characteristics of the city government that often are most praised—its representativeness and openness with respect to interest groups that want a say in decision making—frustrate the capacity of the government to use information for, and even to make, decisions.[13]

If the conclusion regarding the city government's ability to make the most productive use of improved labor market information is not optimistic, a somewhat different picture emerges with respect to the potential that improved labor market information holds for the city's nongovernmental intermediaries. In the first place, businesses and unions, far more than the city government, have relatively clear perceptions of their roles in the local economy and, generally speaking, evidence internal organizational structures that are more stable and well-defined than the government's. Officials of a major corporation or labor union, for example, face fewer problems than city government officials in arriving at some form of consensus regarding information, not only with respect to determining the sort of information they need but in interpreting the information they acquire. In addition, nongovernmental leaders generally possess a degree of decision-making freedom not shared by their counterparts in city government. From a variety of perspectives, private organizations are generally better equipped than governmental organizations—particularly governments as fragmented as New York City's—to use information.

Second, there are indications that businesses and unions in New York City are reacting to changes in the local environment that will facilitate their capacity to use information about the labor market more efficiently. The city's four year employment decline, which began in 1969, seems to have increased the business community's awareness that business must play a more active role in the city's economic and political processes. Furthermore, the shared interests of the business community are increasingly receiving recognition in organizational concerns. The chairman of one leading business group proposed in 1973 at a meeting of business association leaders that business groups in New York City coordinate their research, manpower, and planning efforts "to develop a unified policy for the improvement of New York City."[4] If the city's economy continues to evidence significant problems, it is likely that the business community will become better integrated than in the past.

A third important development that might upgrade both the quality and effectiveness of labor market information concerns the growing recognition by the city's unions, particularly in the private sector, of the necessity of greater cooperation with business in order to protect the interests of the labor unions themselves. If the relationship between business and labor in certain sectors of the economy becomes less conflictive and more cooperative (and this seems to be occurring), improved labor market information can play a significant role in enabling businesses and unions even better to adjust their relationship. This improvement alone could have a significant impact on the future of the city's economy.

CONTINUING RESEARCH IN URBAN LABOR MARKET INFORMATION

Interest in upgrading labor market information is spurred by the premise that information users, whether direct or indirect participants, can translate improved information into improved decisions that will enhance the efficiency of labor markets. Nothing in this study suggests that improving information would be dysfunctional, but much suggests that realizing the linkage between improved information and improved labor markets in a city like New York will be difficult.

In order to improve the stock of labor market information in New York City the major challenge is to improve the supply-demand relationship between those who produce and those who use labor market information. This linkage is poorly developed at present. In an ideal setting the best way to improve this linkage, perhaps, would be to centralize the production function. Centralization would minimize repetitive analysis, which is considerable at present, and reduce the overall costs of information production. Furthermore, in an age of increasingly sophisticated computer techniques, one central repository of data would be extremely useful.

In a less complex system than New York City this might be possible, but the absolute number of information users in New York City is probably such that no single production unit could ever be developed that could respond to such varied demands for information. Failing the means for improving the direct link between information production and use, improvements in the existing information base will probably have to come about from improved collection and transmission of existing data. The complexity of the local environment dictates an incremental, gradual approach to improving labor market information.

Assuming that better labor market information can be realized, the ways it is utilized by labor market intermediaries will largely determine the benefits to be realized from better information. Again, our attention is directed more to those who use information than to information itself. The decision-making, information-utilizing behavior of intermediaries is not uniform—at least not in New York City. The evolving character of the city government the single most important labor market participant, does not provide much hope that it will quickly prove to be an adept information user.* However, this conclusion would not seem warranted with respect to the city's nongovernmental intermediaries. Their evolving relationships—again, a function of changes occurring within the local economy—suggest that their capacity to utilize information is increasing and will continue to increase.

Viewing urban labor market information as a dependent variable intimately related to certain economic characteristics (and social and political characteristics as well) of an urban system, it seems that continuing research in urban labor market information should focus on comparative analysis, not only of large metropolitan areas such as New York City but of smaller, more homogeneous urban areas as well.

One critically important area for comparative analysis is concerned with the importance of information in various urban environments. Is it more important for intermediaries in one economic system than it is for those in another to possess good labor market information? If New York City had fewer nongovernmental participants, if the city's employers and workers were not engaged in such a broad variety of productive enterprises, and if the city's economy were not changing so rapidly, better information about the local labor market would be easier to obtain—but information might not be so important.

If it is indeed the case that improving the quality and use of information is more important in a complex economy like New York City's than in a less complex economy, the relationship between the importance of information and the structural complexity observed in this study suggests a disturbing hypothesis: In those urban systems for which information is more important, information will prove more difficult to acquire and use, and in those systems for which information is less important, information will prove easier to acquire and use. If this hypothesis is correct, New York City's informational weaknesses are most unfortunate, and efforts to improve the quality of information should be speeded up. On an a priori basis it would seem that quality information is more important in a dynamic, constantly changing economy than in a more stable economy. The behavior of labor market actors in New York City, who voice considerable concern over information weaknesses but have not yet mounted a concerted effort to upgrade labor market information, suggests that their benefit-cost calculations weigh against the importance of upgrading information. This lack of concern for better information could be very shortsighted.

------

*This conclusion will be particularly true if the city government is restructured because of the considerable pressure for political decentralization.

A second area that this study suggests as ripe for comparative analysis concerns the ability of various local governments to use information effectively. Do decentralized municipal governments, such as those in New York City and Los Angeles, evidence less information-using capacity than more centralized metropolitan governments such as Chicago's?* If so, do centralized governments acquire a broad spectrum of information, or is the supposed capacity of centralized governments to use information merely a reflection of the fact that they may generate or receive for consideration less labor market information?

A third major research concern should be to identify differences in existing information networks in cities with different economic and labor market characteristics. Are information linkages more developed in smaller cities? What effect does economic diversity have on information linkages? Do metropolitan areas with cohesive business (or union) communities tend to develop better, more complete labor market information than communities in which the principal nongovernmental actors are fragmented? Answers to these questions might shed light on certain policy issues related to improving labor market information in large metropolitan areas. For example, evidence that businesses and unions in other cities, acting separately or conjointly, can significantly improve labor market information might suggest that greater reliance should be placed on the nongovernmental sector than on government in attempting to improve labor market information.

The role of labor market information in an urban environment is something about which very little is known, particularly with respect to the ability of key intermediaries to use information as a resource for change (or as a resource for controlling change). New York City's major labor market intermediaries operate in a complex network of change to which they must continually react; many of the change variables that impact on the city are beyond the ability of intermediaries to affect—except marginally, perhaps. The city is not a closed system but an open subsystem.

Information is a resource, not an abstraction. It is costly to obtain and difficult to use. That much is known. How important information is, compared to other change variables, is not well understood. A long tradition of thought and experience suggests that good information plays an important role in creating equilibrium in economic (and political) relationships. To the extent that participants in an open economic system suffer from inadequate information, one can strongly presume that their interactions will not be optimized. This study in no way disputes that presumption.

---

*The hypothesis would be, of course, that a centralized political system uses information more efficiently than a decentralized political system. A comparative analysis of Chicago and New York City would be instructive, particularly with respect to the governmental component, because both economies are large, diversified, and changing.

143

NOTES

1. "Pension Bill is Passed in Both Houses," *New York Times*, July 27, 1973, p. 1.

2. See Yavitz and Morse, *The Labor Market: An Information System* (New York: Praeger, 1973), pp. 42-44. The authors emphasize that the functional responsibilities of information users generally determine the characteristics of requisite information.

3. See, for example, U.S. Department of Labor, Bureau of Labor Statistics, Middle Atlantic Regional Office, *The Current Social and Economic Scene in New York,* (Washington, D.C.: Government Printing Office, March 1973), pp. 7-9.

4. See, for example, New York State Department of Commerce, *New York State Business Fact Book*, 1972-73 edition.

5. The New York City Rand Institute, *Changing Patterns of Employment in the New York Metropolitan Area* (New York: New York Rand Institute, December 1971).

6. "City Lags in Payroll Hikes," *New York Post*, March 14, 1973, p. 16.

7. Yavitz and Morse, op. cit., pp. 63-72.

8. Jay Forrester, *Urban Dynamics* (Cambridge, Mass.: MIT Press, 1969), p. 113.

9. Wilbur Thompson's *A Preface to Urban Economics* (Baltimore: The Johns Hopkins Press, 1965) represents an earlier attempt at building a series of theoretical generalizations about the nexus between urban economies and urban political systems, but Thompson's work remains undeveloped and no other important theoretical works have emerged.

10. Boris Yavitz and Dean W. Morse, "Labor Market Information" in Eli Ginzberg et al., eds., *New York is Very Much Alive,* (New York: McGraw-Hill, 1973), p. 233.

11. Ibid.

12. Ibid., p. 232.

13. For an illuminating discussion of precisely this point, see Wallace Sayre and Herbert Kaufman, *Governing New York City,* (New York: Norton, 1965), pp. 716-725.

14. "Business Groups Urged to Aid City," *New York Times*, May 23, 1973, p. 43.

8

CONCLUSIONS
AND POLICY
RECOMMENDATIONS

The diverse studies comprising this book lead to numerous and varied policy recommendations with respect to the role and usefulness of labor market information in the urban economy. In this chapter we summarize the major conclusions of each of these studies and derive from them proposals for improving the usefulness of labor market information for, respectively, ex-offenders (and other previously institutionalized persons), vocational training and public education institutions, and major actors in the New York City economy. We then identify the commonalities among the findings and policy recommendations of these studies (remaining, however, cognizant of the characteristics peculiar to the environments and settings from which they derive), indicating how attention to them may improve labor market information systems and, ultimately, the utilization of human resources in the urban economy.

Our first study began with a review of manpower programs for offenders; we found that the services provided in those programs had little discernible impact on the labor market experiences of offenders who were subsequently released. On the one hand, our findings are surprising, considering that most offender manpower programs were made operational during a period of sustained economic expansion in which the existence of tight labor markets led to expectations of programmatic "success." On the other hand, the static conception underlying virtually all those programs—a conception that ignored the dynamics of institutionalization and the labor market—does not promise much in the way of positive impacts for ex-offenders. Further, the failure to integrate evaluation into the design of offender manpower programs and the conceptual and methodological limitations on existing evaluations do not permit wide (or perhaps even narrow) generalizations about the efficacy of these programs.[1]

Our analysis also demonstrated that the bulk of job opportunities available to ex-offenders in New York City and its environs are concentrated in "secondary" labor markets and that information about such opportunities is transmitted largely through informal rather than formal channels. In the information conveyance process and in the search for work presumably encouraged by such information, a key role is played by intermediaries that serve essentially as labor market surrogates for ex-offenders. These intermediaries aid and, in some cases, substitute for the formerly institutionalized in their intensive search for employment along the corridors of the local labor market. Unfortunately, the ability of ex-offenders to obtain (and retain) work or to continue looking for work, even when supplemented by activities of various intermediaries, is powerfully constrained by the system of manpower utilization dominant in incarcerative institutions—a system that differs from and promotes individual behaviors antithetical to those in more conventional worlds of work.

The principal implication of these findings for labor market information is probably that information per se is a relatively marginal component among the many other factors that affect the labor market experiences of ex-offenders and, more generally, the formerly institutionalized in the urban economy. Continued de-emphasis on institutionalization as a way of dealing with "deviant" behavior,[2] alteration of patterns of manpower utilization in total institutions, and consideration of institutionalization as a dynamic, multi-faceted flow process in the formation of manpower programs or other rehabilitation efforts, appear more likely to aid the institutionalized than manipulations of labor market information systems, especially formal systems. This does not mean, however, that labor market information has no utility for ex-offenders in New York City, or that the collection, dissemination, and utilization of such information cannot be improved.

For example, a current listing of employers who willingly hire ex-offenders would be of considerable value to released prisoners, as would detailed specification of wages and working conditions offered by these employers. Such information is not now collected by any agency or employment service, public or private, and, moreover, it is doubtful that it can be obtained at all. Employers generally claim a proprietary interest in the jobs they offer, "advertising" but a few of the characteristics of their employments when they search for workers. (Indeed, the question of so-called managerial prerogatives needs further explicit consideration in discussions of and policies aimed at improving the employability of the formerly institutionalized.) Even those employers who occasionally or regularly hire former prisoners who are referred to them by an employment agency, community institution, or personal friend, perhaps, are reluctant to disseminate widely their willingness to employ ex-convicts. Indeed, this reticence on the part of employers combined with the inability of public and private agencies to secure relevant employment data of the type described above partially accounts for the role of family and friends, community institutions, and other intermediaries in the job search activities of released offenders who enter the New York City labor market. Thus, a recommendation that employment agencies search out job market data directly relevant to ex-offenders or other formerly institutionalized persons—a recommendation we support—should not create strong expectations of "success."

Improvements in the labor market experiences of former prisoners are more likely to come about from a broadening of the concept of information rather than through more intensive attempts to collect and disseminate information narrowly defined. Specifically, the counseling, support, and job placement services now offered to ex-offenders largely by family and friends, some community institutions, and probation and parole officers need to be recognized as components of labor market information, much as knowledge of job opportunities and accompanying wages and working conditions are now regarded. Given the characteristics of the institutional dynamic described earlier, it is the intensive support, counseling and placement activities that are especially germane to ex-offenders and that play a prominent role in determining employment experiences subsequent to release. This analysis leads to the recommendation that public and private agencies take cognizance of the role of critical intermediaries in aiding ex-offenders and other formerly institutionalized persons and provide to those intermediaries the extensive but narrowly-defined information they possess about job opportunities in the local labor market. The various intermediaries can then seek further information from employers about these job opportunities, and can then link their counseling, support and placement services directly to them. (In the absence of such information, intermediaries focus largely on the attitudinal characteristics and psychological adjustment of ex-offenders.) Implementation of our recommendation, in addition to providing a focal point for the dissemination of labor market information by public and private agencies, would strengthen the role of intermediaries in aiding ex-offenders and cause intermediaries to place greater emphasis than they now do on economic and labor market considerations as they affect the "rehabilitation" of criminal offenders.

Finally, an even further broadening of informational concepts suggests that public and private agencies should gather and transmit to various interest groups and decision-making bodies their knowledge (that is, information) about legal and other structural barriers in order to improve the labor market experiences of released prisoners. In Chapter 3 we reviewed the way in which licensing and personnel policies operate to eliminate many occupations and even entire industries as potential sources of employment for ex-offenders. Yet, as the evidence now available indicates that such requirements for and restrictions on entry do not bear any relationship to ability to perform a job and, consequently, unfairly discriminate against those who are excluded from the occupations and industries in question, we recommend to public policy makers that a labor market information system, especially a local system, include mechanisms for investigating and disseminating information on artificial restrictions on labor supplies to specific employments, occupations, and industries. Implementation of this recommendation could result, we believe, in the opening of at least some primary labor market opportunities to released prisoners and other formerly institutionalized persons in U.S. society.

Our second study explored the ways in which New York City's training and educational institutions have used labor market information in program planning, curriculum development, and student guidance activities. On balance, for a variety of reasons, the informational impact in these areas can best be described as minimal.

First, a significant body of opinion among administrators of educational institutions holds that course offerings and, more generally, programs of

147

instruction, should not be dictated, perhaps even no more than nominally affected, by current or future labor market conditions. From this perspective, freedom of individual choice is weighted more heavily than institutional preferences in response to the vagaries of the local labor market.[3] This position derives from a basic philosophical view neither easily changed nor readily reconcilable with notions about the primacy of labor market information.

A second factor limiting the use of labor market information by vocational education administrators is the increasing tendency for program graduates to go on to college rather than seek immediate employment. Thus, vocational education is now more commonly viewed as an alternative developmental pattern rather than as a necessary investment that must be closely linked to local labor market conditions. Even for those who do enter the labor market immediately upon completion of high school, however, in the opinion of program administrators, job placements need not be directly related to training. Such training, they argue, is a lifetime investment of which graduates can make differential use as labor market conditions change, and, further, the general work habits and attitudes inculcated during training will serve the trainee in various work capacities.

Finally, the effective use of local labor market information by New York City's educational and training institutions is limited by the decentralized administrative structures characteristic of their programs. At each level—high school, undergraduate, graduate, and adult training—decentralized administration complicates (and, in some cases, prevents) the planning of programs, the structuring of curricula, and the coordination of educational and vocational training efforts. The atomistic nature of these administrative structures is a given that must be confronted both by those who devise and operate labor market information systems and by those who argue for the increased utility of information generated by such systems.

Much as ex-offenders, students enrolled in vocational training programs in New York City rely more on family and personal acquaintances than on local agencies for the information upon which they base their work and career decisions. Similarly, responsible officials of the city government's education and training institutions turn to their own sources of information on present and future work opportunities more often than they rely on data supplied by local agencies. They do this in part because the government agencies (the Regional Office of the U.S. Department of Labor and the New York State Employment Service) are not in a position to provide reliable, detailed labor market information, though their aggregate data concerning job openings and employment levels are useful. Thus, consideration of individual and institutional decision-making processes in the education and vocational training settings again cautions against overexaggeration of the usefulness of labor market information, especially that derived from formal informational systems.

Despite these caveats, labor market information can contribute to the experiences of people who enroll in New York City's educational and training institutions, and it can especially improve their career choices. Those who leave high school before graduation, for example, should be better informed about the consequences of such an act, the options it potentially forecloses, and the various reentry routes by which access may be gained to adult training, equivalency diplomas, employment assistance, or simply returning to school. For those who graduate high school and enter the labor market directly, informational services and job opportunities are more readily available, but these could be more closely allied with the graduate's interests and training than they are now. More detailed information about apprenticeship programs, career paths in internal labor markets, and higher-ranking jobs to which access may be gained through selected (and often not clearly visible) ports of entry would be especially useful to the high school graduate. Those who graduate high school and go on to college at one of the CUNY campuses require improved information about the variety of programs offered at the different campuses and the opportunities available for transfering between campuses, especially in view of the concentration of students in the senior rather than the community colleges in the CUNY system. Finally, those who drop out of college and into the labor market after a brief exposure to higher education might gain more than most others from labor market information. Such information should be tied to the degree of finality of the student's decision (that is, to a determination of whether he is leaving school temporarily or permanently) and can also be used to assuage some of the career expectiations that might have been raised by even brief exposure to college education but that must be tempered in view of the decision to leave school. In sum the information most useful for the groups discussed here is the sort that allows them to keep their options open and facilitates their movement between work and nonwork activities or between work and various other institutions, notably education and training institutions.

As with released offenders, however, better labor market information will not suffice to improve the job choice or career planning of those who enter the New York City labor market after exposure to one or more of the city government's educational or vocational training programs. This information (and other data typically not regarded as information) is transmitted to students and trainees by critical intermediaries—family and friends, guidance counselors, program planners, placement officers, and training directors—some of whom staff the various training and educational institutions. These intermediaries play key roles in aiding the student to choose from among a wide assortment of course offerings and training programs, in counseling the dropout or graduate about work opportunities, and in guiding young people in selecting and planning for a career path. Providing of labor market information directly to these intermediaries would enable them to link their critical counseling, guidance, and placement functions to job opportunities in the labor market and would strengthen the supportive institutions that house these intermediaries. As before, this requires a broadening of received concepts of information. Here, too, moreover, a broadened informational system can include a mechanism for investigating and disseminating information about artificial restrictions on labor supply to various occupations. In contrast to bars on the employment of ex-offenders, which impact upon relatively few persons in U.S. society, the requirement of high school graduation for entry into numerous jobs, for example, affects the work experience, earnings, and mobility of millions of people.[4] Consequently, the findings of our second study, also identifying the limits to conventional labor market information

149

(and informational systems), again lead us to recommend a substantial broadening of informational concepts.

Our third study focused on the uses of labor market information by major actors in the New York City economy—employers, trade unions, and municipal government. Special attention was given to the linkages between local government and the local economy as manifested in education, employment, manpower training, economic development, and service delivery. This study concluded that improved labor market information is likely to have no more than a marginal impact on the decision processes of the city's employers, trade unions, and municipal government.

Consider, first, that information is regarded by the parties who trade on it as a power resource to aid in the achievement of an objective, especially when competing interest groups are involved. The kind of information called into play and the manner in which it is obtained, analyzed, and traded are determined individually by the major actors in the urban economy. Collective bargaining between New York City's municipal government and its major public employee unions best illustrates this process, perhaps,[5] but numerous examples of it are available in other contexts. Suffice it to say that what represents "information" to one party among the major interest groups active in a complex and dynamic urban economy might differ substantially from the "information" most relevant to another party.

A second factor limiting the potential usefulness of improved information in the urban labor market is the essentially political nature of many major decisions made in or about the metropolitan economy. Decisions concerning the building of a new convention center, expansion of the Public Employment Program, construction or refurbishing of an expressway, decentralization of public school administration, or the preservation of recreational areas and even neighborhood patterns—issues about which major decisions have been made in New York City within the last decade—are not based centrally (or perhaps even marginally) on information about their utility, consequences or, more formally, costs and benefits; instead, they are based on the ability of competing interest groups to develop the organizational skills necessary to the formation of a "winning" coalition. This, the epitome of the political process, depends to only the slightest degree on labor market information. Indeed, when one of the actors involved in a major decision about the local economy is concerned with labor market information, he is likely to seek it through a specialized intermediary (for example, a trade association or research staff of a national union) rather than directly from government. Here, the utilization of labor market information parallels that evidenced by ex-offenders and vocational training institutions. (This observation underscores the limits to the utilization of labor market information derived from formal informational systems—limits heretofore most commonly associated with individual job search.)

Finally, the usefulness of existing or improved labor market information for key decision makers in the urban economy is limited by the fractionalized administrative structure characteristic of the city's major actor, namely its municipal government. Our analysis of public education, manpower training, service delivery, and even economic development in New York City showed how responsibility for each of these functions is dispersed among numerous

150

independent and quasi-independent agencies, how these agencies compete for information with each other, and how they resist sharing such information with counterpart agencies or other departments of city government. Competition between the City Planning Commission and the Board of Estimate over the evolution and planning of New York City's economy is but one example of the ways that labor market information becomes submerged within larger administrative—and political—forces. When the demands of increasingly well-organized local community groups and those of traditionally well-organized industry and labor spokesmen are added to the decentralized, intracompetitive form of governmental administration in New York City, there emerges a political dynamic in which decisions reached are at best only tangentially related to labor market information. Hence, the basis for our judgment that improved information is likely to have but a minor impact on major actors in the urban economy of New York City.

As before, a judgment that labor market information is not of central importance to decision makers—in this case, major actors in the urban economy—does not mean that such information cannot be upgraded or that it cannot contribute to improved decisions. It does suggest, however, that any effort to improve systematically the quantity and quality of labor market information must be made generally within the same environment that has shaped the existing information network. The starting point for constructing an improved information system in New York City is to recognize that an enormous amount of useful information already exists and probably will continue to be produced, albeit in an expensive, often haphazard manner. Whereas informational problems were earlier explained as being due largely to incomplete meshing of production and use, poor distribution of information no doubt substantially contributes to the widely-held view that labor market information available in New York City is inadequate. Improving the distribution of information is a far easier task than integrating its production and use, except in those instances in which information is generated in a private buyer-seller relationship. But many important information producers—academicians, specialized research groups, and government agencies—aggregatively generate large amounts of information whose distribution is in no way constrained by the need to protect commercial relationships.

This important characteristic of the existing information network suggests the desirability of creating a variant of the "clearinghouse" concept already in operation in legal, banking, and other circles. A clearinghouse organization might at least sell (or be subsidized to provide) information about information; it could at best actually sell or otherwise provide labor market information in either abstract or nonabridged form. While it is unlikely that such an enterprise could tap into much of the information presently generated in the private marketplace, a clearinghouse could easily acquire information generated by those with no vested interest in maintaining privacy of knowledge. That no such organizational entity exists today in the city does not imply that its utility would be marginal; the absence of such an organization might suggest, however, that government has a role to play in its development and support. Considering the huge sums of money currently invested in information by both the private and public sectors (not to mention the even larger sums of public and private

151

money invested in social programs framed in the absence of adequate information), an experiment with the clearinghouse concept seems a reasonable investment, particularly in light of the pervasive and as yet undisputed assumption that improved information plays a positive role in planning and decision-making processes.*

A variant of the clearinghouse notion is the consortium approach developed by Yavitz and Morse discussed briefly in Chapter 7.[6] They elaborate the ways that local consortia of major information users might be organized and, through the adroit application of a pricing system, might move beyond the storage and transmission of existing data (the clearinghouse concept) to "custom-made" analysis of data for individual users. The introduction of a clearinghouse-consortium approach in a way that would neither compete with nor weaken the existing market for manpower and economic information would benefit those information users who, by dint of limited resources, or because they only occasionally need information, are unable to benefit from in-house or external information sources. While major businesses may well continue to internally generate or externally purchase information for their own purposes, smaller business associations—and even individuals—would benefit from the service provided by an information clearinghouse.

Assuming that nongovernmental actors would realize the most important benefits of the clearinghouse approach the problem of improving the information base for government planners, of course, remains. We recommend as an incremental reform the creation within the government of New York City of a unit charged with the sole responsibility of putting the local government's information house in order. The initial charge of such a unit would be two-fold: a) to locate, collect, and provide mechanisms for dissemination of the considerable amount of information that various agencies have already produced, and b) to "retrieve" information now stored in the separate automatic data processing systems of the city government. Again, our major assumption is not that information for government planners is wholly inadequate but, rather, that such information—particularly that produced by agencies charged with economic and human resource development responsibilities—is poorly distributed.

It appears at present a difficult charge for a city government information unit to go beyond general information dissemination and retrieval functions to "custom-made" analysis for city government agencies. Staffs in the various line and overhead agencies in New York City have in recent years acquired considerable familiarity with specific information needs and data-gathering techniques. Maintaining a decentralized system of information production but facilitating improved dissemination of information through a single centralized agency seems a sensible and, importantly, workable alternative, comparable to arrangements found in the private sector.

---

*This assumption and others related to it are being examined in a forthcoming study of informational systems for management and planning being conducted by Alfred S. Eichner and Charles Brecher under the sponsorship of the Conservation of Human Resources Project, Columbia University.

The most obvious location for such an agency is within the office of the mayor. The mayor of New York City perennially suffers from the absence of labor market and other types of information, yet he remains the most important locus of power and responsibility with respect to economic and manpower development in the city government. If the disabling features of political fragmentation in the planning and policy processes in New York City are to be at least partially overcome, it is necessary that the mayor's hand be strengthened. Improving the mayor's information base will aid in solidifying his role in the developmental process.

Given the complexity of New York City, the temptation is great to suggest that the development of a comprehensive labor market information system is utopian; given the scope of exogenous and endogenous factors that constrain private and public actors from realizing their developmental goals, the temptation is great to suggest that the benefits to be realized from a comprehensive information system would be minimal. Yet information might reduce complexity through an improvement in understanding, and it might increase local adaptive capacity through an improvement in decision making. For these two reasons, greater emphasis should be placed on improving the city government's information network. The incremental strategy outlined above, built around two new institutional forms—that is intermediaries—whose functions are limited to improving information dissemination, poses few threats to the existing information network and requires no huge commitment of resources. It is a modest, experimental proposal consistent with the viewpoint, often expressed in this book, that labor market information has limits as well as uses.

The studies contained in this volume are in many ways disparate; certainly, they focus on different units of analysis. Nevertheless, the findings and policy recommendations derived from each contain important commonalities with respect to the utilization of labor market information in the urban economy.

First, the studies take issue with the view that better labor market information will automatically lead to improved individual and institutional decision making. Whether we consider ex-offenders or other formerly institutionalized persons, vocational training and educational institutions, or major actors in the urban economy, decision-making processes are complex and responsive to a variety of forces. Within these multivariate decision-making matrices, labor market information per se appears as a relatively minor component. The collection, processing, dissemination and utilization of such information occurs in an environment in which fundamental social political and economic forces are at work and, consequently, in which decisions about job choice, training programs, or economic development depend heavily on power relations, attitudes, employment practices, job availabilities, and the like. Consequently, labor market information operates (enters) largely at the margins of decision making, being powerfully constrained by more fundamental forces.

Second, information that informs the decisions of individuals, institutions, and major actors in an urban economy such as that of New York City rarely flows directly from producer to user. Instead, information is typically filtered

153

through and, in some cases, fundamentally altered by critical intermediaries prior to its distribution and use by the final decision maker. While the intermediaries most relevant to ex-offenders seeking employment in the urban economy are not the same as those affecting the curriculum decisions of vocational training programs and public educational institutions (or their students), and these differ from the intermediaries who most directly impinge upon the decisions of employers, unions, and the municipal government in a city, each acts as a conduit through which presumably objective, neutral information must pass before a decision is reached. These intermediaries not only transmit information, of course, but also filter, augment, subtract from, and shape it; in other words, ultimately they determine what gets passed on to whom, helping to shape the ways that information will be used. Formal informational systems, or most models of them, too frequently assume that information passes easily and impersonally from source to user and thereby effectuates a matching process that in the aggregate improves the functioning of labor (or "product") markets. The findings of the present study urge us to modify this view and to recognize if not incorporate critical intermediaries into models of labor market or other information systems.[7] Cognizance should also be taken of the frequently informal nature of information networks in which intermediaries are most likely to operate and thus of the limits on the utility of formal information systems that gives rise to this observation.

Finally, our numerous and varied policy recommendations commonly suggest a strengthening of linkages among formal information systems, critical intermediaries, and ultimate decision makers in the labor market. In particular, we need to know more about the role played by intermediaries in the decision processes of various individuals, groups, and institutions—including those considered in this volume—in the urban economy. With this knowledge we will be better able to link existing labor market information, derived largely from formal informational systems, to the supportive institutions and services that so fundamentally affect and inform part of the decision-making processes of key labor market principals. Out of this effort, we believe, will emerge "significant improvements in the development and utilization of the nation's human resources."[8]

NOTES

1. In the role of evaluation in social experimentation generally, see Alice M. Rivlin, "Social Experiments: Promise and Problems," *Science*, 183 (January 11, 1974)

2. Such de-emphasis requires, in turn, a strengthening of supportive institutions. For an example of the consequences that may result when such supportive institutions and services are not available, see Murray Schumach, "Where Can Mental Patients Go?" *New York Times*, February 24, 1974, Part IV, p. 5.

3. For analysis of this issue on a broader scale, see Walter A. Fogel and Daniel J. B. Mitchell, "Higher Education Decision Making and the Labor

Market," in *Higher Education and the Labor Market*, Margaret S. Gordon, ed. (New York: McGraw-Hill and the Carnegie Commission on Higher Education, 1974).

4. See Ivar Berg, *Education and Jobs: The Great Training Robbery* (New York: Praeger, 1970), passim: Hirsch S. Ruchlin, "Education as a Labor Market Variable," *Industrial Relations*, 10 (October 1971): 287-300; Walter A. Fogel, "Mexical Americans in Southwest Labor Markets," *Mexican American Study Project* (Los Angeles: Division of Research, Graduate School of Business Administration, University of California, Los Angeles, October 1967), esp. Ch. 7.

5. This dynamic is more fully analyzed in Raymond D. Horton, *Municipal Labor Relations in New York City: Lessons of the Lindsay-Wagner Years* (New York: Praeger, 1973).

6. See Boris Yavitz and Dean W. Morse, *The Labor Market: An Information System* (New York: Praeger, 1973), Chs. 9, 10.

7. The findings of other studies also suggest a modified view. Compare with Joseph C. Ullman and George P. Huber, "Are Job Banks Improving the Labor Market Information System?" *Industrial and Labor Relations Review*, 27 (January 1974): 171-85.

8. Eli Ginzberg, "Foreword," in David Lewin, et al., *The Urban Labor Market: Institutions, Information, Linkages* (forthcoming), p. 11.

ABOUT THE AUTHORS

DAVID LEWIN is Associate Professor at Columbia University's Graduate School of Business, and Research Associate at the Conservation of Human Resources Project. He is the author of several articles dealing with public sector labor relations which have appeared in *Industrial Relations, Industrial and Labor Relations Review, Public Administration Review,* and *Public Personnel Management.*

Dr. Lewin holds a B.S. from California State, M.B.A. from California and Ph.D. from California.

RAYMOND D. HORTON is Associate Professor at Columbia University's Graduate School of Business, and Research Associate at the Conservation of Human Resources Project. Dr. Horton is the author of *Municipal Labor Relations in New York City: Lessons of the Lindsay-Wagner Years* (New York: Praeger, 1973).

Dr. Horton holds a B.A. from Grinnell College, L.L.B. from Harvard University and Ph.D. from Columbia University.

ROBERT SHICK is currently a Quantitative Analyst at the Human Resources Administration of the City of New York where he is involved in program planning and analysis. He was a Research Associate at the Conservation of Human Resources Project and is an assistant author of the book *Unemployment in the Urban Core: An Analysis of Thirty Cities with Policy Recommendations* (New York: Praeger, 1972) by Stanley L. Friedlander.

Mr. Shick holds a B.S. from the City College of New York and M.A. in economics from Indiana University.

CHARLES BRECHER has been a Research Associate at the Conservation of Human Resources Project since 1968. He is the author of *Where Have All the Dollars Gone?* (New York: Praeger, 1974), *The Impact of Federal Antipoverty Policies* (New York: Praeger, 1973), *Upgrading the Blue Collar and Service Workers* (Baltimore: The John Hopkins Press, 1972) and a co-author of two books by Eli Ginzberg and the Conservation of Human Resources staff, *Urban Health Services: The Case of New York* (New York: Columbia University Press, 1971) and *New York Is Very Much Alive: A Manpower View* (New York: McGraw-Hill, 1973).

Dr. Brecher holds a Ph.D. in Political Science from the City University of New York and a B.A. degree with Honors from the University of Florida.

EMPLOYMENT EXPANSION AND METROPOLITAN TRADE

> A Conservation of Human Resources Study
> Richard Victor Knight
> Foreword by Eli Ginzberg

THE LABOR MARKET: An Information System

> A Conservation of Human Resources Study
> Boris Yavitz and Dean W. Morse, with Anna B. Dutka
> Foreword by Eli Ginzberg

NEW DIRECTIONS IN EMPLOYABILITY: Reducing Barriers to Full
Employment

> Edited by David B. Orr

PRIVATE ASSUMPTION OF PUBLIC RESPONSIBILITIES: The Role
of Urban Business in Urban Manpower Programs

> Peter Kobrak

UNEMPLOYMENT IN THE URBAN CORE: An Analysis of Thirty
Cities with Policy Recommendations

> A Conservation of Human Resources Study
> Stanley Friedlander, assisted by Robert Schick
> Foreword by Eli Ginzberg

WHERE HAVE ALL THE DOLLARS GONE?: Public Expenditures for
Human Resources Development in New York City, 1961-71

> A Conservation of Human Resources Study
> Charles Brecher
> Foreword by Eli Ginzberg